ALSO BY PHILLIP LOPATE

*Portrait Inside My Head*

*At the End of the Day*

*Notes on Sontag*

*Two Marriages*

*American Movie Critics: An Anthology From the Silents Until Now*

*Waterfront: A Journey around Manhattan*

*Rudy Burckhardt*

*Getting Personal: Selected Writings*

*Writing New York: A Literary Anthology*

*Totally, Tenderly, Tragically*

*Portrait of My Body*

*The Art of the Personal Essay: An Anthology from the Classical Era to the Present*

*Against Joie de Vivre*

*The Rug Merchant*

*Bachelorhood: Tales of the Metropolis*

*Confessions of Summer*

*The Daily Round*

*The Eyes Don't Always Want to Stay Open*

*Being with Children: A High-Spirited Personal Account of Teaching Writing, Theater, and Videotape*

# PHILLIP LOPATE

# TO SHOW AND TO TELL

## The Craft of Literary Nonfiction

FREE PRESS

*New York London Toronto Sydney New Delhi*

Free Press
A Division of Simon & Schuster, Inc.
1230 Avenue of the Americas
New York, NY 10020

First Free Press trade paperback edition February 2013

FREE PRESS and colophon are trademarks of Simon & Schuster, Inc.

For information about special discounts for bulk purchases, please contact
Simon & Schuster Special Sales at 1-866-506-1949 or
business@simonandschuster.com.

The Simon & Schuster Speakers Bureau can bring authors to your live event. For
more information or to book an event contact the Simon & Schuster Speakers
Bureau at 1-866-248-3049 or visit our website at www.simonspeakers.com.

"Voice" by Run Padgett, from *Toujours l'amour* copyright 1976. Used by
permission of the author.

*Book design by Ellen R. Sasahara*

Manufactured in the United States of America

7  9  10  8

Library of Congress Cataloging-in-Publication Data

Lopate, Phillip.
To show and to tell : the craft of literary nonfiction /
by Phillip Lopate. — 1st Free Press trade paperback ed.
p. cm.
1. Creative nonfiction—Authorship. 2. Autobiography—Authorship.
3. Essay—Authorship. 4. Prose literature—Authorship. I. Title.
PN145.L67 2013
808.02—dc23
2012025669

ISBN: 978-1-4516-9632-5
ISBN: 978-1-4516-9633-2 (ebook)

# Contents

# II.

## Studies of Practitioners 133

# Introduction

I should explain straight-out that I consider myself to be as much a teacher as a writer. It's not simply that a good deal of my annual income derives from teaching; it's also that I find it a fascinating challenge, one that nourishes my psyche—and my own writing. Many of my fellow writers treat teaching as a lower calling; they only do it to pay the rent, or until such time as they can support themselves entirely from royalties and advances. For my part, I think I would continue to teach even if I were to win the lottery. I find myself needing to articulate responses on the spot to any and all questions put me by students and their manuscripts, regardless of how much I may feel myself to be bluffing. I am also intrigued whenever I encounter resistance to my advice. Since I tend to doubt myself and my wisdom, I even feel some sympathy with those who want to question my prescriptions, though that does not stop me in the least from continuing to offer them.

Ever since my anthology *The Art of the Personal Essay* appeared, I have been looked to, rightly or wrongly, as a spokesperson for the essay, and for "creative nonfiction" or "literary nonfiction" (call it what you will) in general. I have been asked to speak at campuses and conferences across the country, and invariably I have been confronted with certain questions—formal, strategic, and ethical—that seem to issue from an insistent anxiety or perplexity. Some of these questions have to do with the borderline between fiction and nonfiction or with the freedom to invent, appropriate, or embroider—what I've come to regard as "law and order issues." When this debate cropped up, my first impulse was to throw up my hands and say the whole controversy has been blown out of proportion and bores me, because it does not speak to where I live as a nonfiction writer (the urge to write the next sentence with as much style and thoughtfulness as I can muster). But I have come to see this neutral response on my part as hypocritical, because I do have opinions on such matters. So I have tried in these pages to explain them, though I hope it will be clear that I am talking about what works for me, not necessarily for everyone.

There are also vexing questions about the ethics of writing about others, particularly family members, intimates, and colleagues. There are questions of technique, such as how do you turn yourself into a character, how do you end an essay, and finally, how do you develop the capacity to think entertainingly and unconventionally on the page? The book's title, *To Show and to Tell*, directly speaks to this last problem by challenging the cliché of writing workshops, "Show, don't tell." I am convinced that both are necessary in literary nonfiction.

What brought me to this conviction was reading older writers: the great personal essayists, memoirists, critics, biographers, and historians of the past. In a sense I am defending here the historical prerogatives of the literary nonfiction form, to charm and entice by way of a voice that can speak in more than one register, that can tell an anecdote, be self-mocking and serious by turns, and analyze a conundrum. My deepest inclination as a writer is historical: to link up what is written today with the rich literary lode of the past. My profoundest belief as a teacher is that many solutions for would-be literary nonfiction writers can be found in the library. To that end, I have included here a long list of exemplary books old and new. I have also included a series of literary case studies—Charles Lamb, William Hazlitt, Ralph Waldo Emerson, James Baldwin, and Edward Hoagland—to explore how nonfiction theory works in practice.

Some of these pieces were commissioned or requested; they may have gotten their start as conference talks, contributions to anthologies, even columns for *Creative Nonfiction* magazine. But they all speak to the same urgent question, of how to write intelligent, satisfying, engaging literary nonfiction.

So who is this book for? On the most basic level, it is for myself, to enable me to work through my thoughts on these questions—and for other nonfiction writers with similar concerns. It is certainly for other teachers of nonfiction and, I would hope, for graduate MFA nonfiction students. It is for what Virginia Woolf called "the common reader," not a critic or scholar but someone who "reads for his own pleasure rather than to impart knowledge or correct the opinions of others." It is meant as well for undergraduate teachers of composition and creative writing—and their students. But it doesn't end there, because the roots of such pedagogical practice extend down to high school, middle school, and even elementary school, where teachers are increasingly being asked to inculcate in their charges the ability to write effective nonfiction.

I feel for these teachers. Third graders are now being asked to write their "memoirs": an invitation which sounds risible, were it not also sensible. It is never too early to know thyself, to begin to interrogate one's experience. The summa of such efforts is the dreaded college application, or "Common App" essay. On the one hand, the Common App essay encourages high school seniors to write with a strong, seductively individual voice, in the classic tradition of the personal essay. On the other hand, the common core curriculum now being implemented for middle and high school students stresses the need to construct an argumentative essay, which stakes a *claim* and supports it. How, then, to balance the adventurousness of an exploratory essay that tracks the author's consciousness and may lead to surprising, original insights, with the need to support a logical argument? Such problems are not irreconcilable, as I have tried to show in "The Essay: Exploration or Argument?"

Believe me, I am thrilled that educators from elementary through secondary schools are starting to place much more emphasis on nonfiction writing. I am less thrilled if it means sacrificing that part of the curriculum formerly devoted to writing stories and poems. Both genres, aside from their innate cultural worth, can be crucial in helping to refine a flexible nonfiction style: fiction, by sharpening the sense of narrative line and character; poetry, by promoting concise language, careful diction, and imaginative use of images and metaphors.

I also have mixed feelings about a certain rigid, mechanistic approach to the evaluation of essays. There are automated systems currently being developed to score middle school and high school test essays, systems which reward long sentences, syntactical complexity, connectors such as "however" or "moreover"—all good things, no doubt, but these robot scorers aren't sensitive enough to gauge original thought, emotional expressiveness, or honesty. We ought to be training young people not just to assert a claim or use bigger words but to think critically—to think against themselves—which may necessitate the abandoning of an original argument or thread for a fruitful digression or self-contradictory ambivalence. In short, the pragmatic justification for learning to write nonfiction effectively should be joined to a renewed respect for the literary traditions that open up extraordinarily ample vistas of interiority, complexity, and stylistic experimentation. My hope is that this book will help to shift the conversation in that direction.

# I.

# THE CRAFT OF
# PERSONAL NARRATIVE

# The State of Nonfiction Today

Nonfiction is sometimes said to be going through a resurgence or an identity crisis, maybe both at the same time, but that is nothing new. Consider the very name of this practice, defined by what it is not: like the Uncola, the Anti-Christ, or antimatter. In the last twenty years some attempt has been made to cloak it with dignity by adding the word "creative" before "nonfiction"; but this is tantamount to saying "*good* poetry." No one sets out to write uncreative nonfiction. I prefer the more traditional-sounding term *literary nonfiction*, though I have to admit that "literary" is also a bit of gratuitous self-praise. The field's boastful insecurity mirrors the literary world's condescending attitude toward it. Every year, the MacArthur, Whiting, Rona Jaffe, Lannan, and Prix de Rome fellowships are announced: a healthy list of fiction writers and poets, and one or two nonfiction writers, if that. When was a Nobel Prize last given to a nonfiction writer?* Personal essay collections, even by such established masters as Edward Hoagland, Nancy Mairs, and Joseph Epstein, are often

---

*Elias Canetti, I suppose, though some would argue he got it for his novel *Auto-da-Fé*.

relegated to a Books in Brief column, as though the genre were merely a dodge to get around writing a *real* book.

Those of us who teach creative writing at universities know that, in the beginning, God created Fiction and Poetry, and saw that it was good. Then some whiners and Satanic misfits started demanding nonfiction courses. In my visits to campuses across the country, I have been approached by graduates stealing up to me like members of an early Christian sect, telling of their struggles to receive the first MFAs for a nonfiction thesis; and even these were often begrudgingly awarded, as though not meant to be a genuine passport, only a visa. Nonfiction writers are the resident aliens of academia.

Yet, curiously, enrollments in nonfiction have held steady, even increased over the years. At first this student interest was attributed to something called "the memoir craze" (note how an interest in autobiographical prose, one of the oldest and most difficult literary practices, can be glibly denigrated as a fad), but when the commercial hoopla about memoirs had settled down, creative writing majors and graduate students continued to seek out nonfiction workshops. I think the main reason is that many students can engage their own reality more confidently than an imagined one. They think they have poor imaginations and therefore are better suited to nonfiction. Eventually they will be disabused of this misconception, when they discover that it takes just as much imagination to construct a meaningful order and context for their lived experiences, and an intriguing personality through which to tell them, as to make up a new set. But meantime, this misunderstanding that nonfiction is easier can be fruitful in attracting candidates to an otherwise daunting task.

Often, no sooner does the would-be nonfiction writer begin to practice his or her craft than a species of "fiction envy" arises. This envy is not surprising when you consider the higher status that fiction holds in the literary pantheon. But even if a student is content with the lower status of nonfiction, she will undoubtedly encounter those creative writing instructors along the way who tell her to "put everything in scenes," for instance, or to use lots of images and sense details, or to stay away from generalities. Here, the more elaborated techniques and rules of the short story workshop have an advantage over the still-evolving pedagogy of nonfiction: they can simply be plugged into a text. When in doubt, make a scene. Many nonfiction instructors today received their training in fiction and had these rules instilled in them. One of the leaders in the nonfiction field, Lee Gutkind, has even specified the goal of creative nonfiction as "trying to write the truth and making it read like a short story or fiction." In an interview with Donna Seaman, he provided this definition: "Creative nonfiction allows the nonfiction writer to use literary techniques usually used only by fiction writers, such as scene-setting, description, dialogue, action, suspense, plot. All those things that make terrific short stories and novels allow the nonfiction writer to tell true stories in the most cinematic and dramatic way possible. That's creative nonfiction."

I don't wish to start a feud, since in some ways I'm in agreement with Gutkind: if he means that a piece of nonfiction should have a plot, suspense, and strong characterization—even character development, in the case of memoir—or if he means that the nonfiction writer should be conscious of constructing an artifice, I'm all for that. But if he means the nonfiction writer should try to render everything in scenes with dialogue and sprinkle sense details everywhere so the text will read as "cinematically" as possible, while staying away from thoughtful analysis because it sounds academic or "abstract," then, no, I don't agree.

For all their shared boundaries, the experiences of fiction and nonfiction are fundamentally different. In the traditional short story or novel, a fictive space is opened up that allows you the reader to disappear into the action, even to the point of forgetting you are reading. In the best nonfiction, it seems to me, you're always made aware that you are being engaged with a supple mind at work. The story line or plot in nonfiction consists of the twists and turns of a thought process working itself out. This is certainly true for the essay, but it is also true, I think, for classic nonfiction in general, be it Thucydides or Pascal or Carlyle, which follows an organizing principle that can be summarized as "tracking the consciousness of the author."

What makes me want to keep reading a nonfiction text is the encounter with a surprising, well-stocked mind as it takes on the challenge of the next sentence, paragraph, and thematic problem it has set for itself. The other element that keeps me reading nonfiction happily is an evolved, entertaining, elegant, or at least highly intentional literary style. The pressure of style should be brought to bear on every passage. "Consciousness plus style equals good nonfiction" is one way of stating the formula.

For me, the great adventure in reading nonfiction is to follow, as I say, a really interesting, unpredictable mind struggling to entangle and disentangle itself in a thorny problem, or even a frivolous problem that is made complex through engagement with a sophisticated mind. George Orwell reflecting on his ambivalence toward Gandhi, Robert Benchley meditating on his face, Seymour Krim on his failure, Susan Sontag on camp, Stendhal on love, Montaigne on experience, Norman Mailer on sex, Virginia Woolf on a room of one's own, Loren Eiseley on brown wasps, Edmund Wilson on the development of socialist thought, Charles Lamb on married couples, Joan Didion on migraines, William Gass on the color blue. . . . None of these examples read like short stories or screenplays; they read like what they are: glorious thought excursions. I have purposely mixed longer, book-length tracts in with smaller essays, to reinforce the point that the pursuit of consciousness is not just the prerogative of the short-sprint personal essayist. Indeed, there is something about consciousness which is almost infinitely extensible—frighteningly so. One thought leads to another, and another, and pretty soon you have Robert Burton's thousand-page *Anatomy of Melancholy*.

George Steiner wrote an essay that he entitled "Ten (Possible) Reasons for the Sadness of Thought." The first reason he gave was that "thought is infinite," though because it is subject to doubt or (to use Steiner's words) "internal contradiction for which there can be no resolution," it is an "incomplete infinity." His second was that thought is uncontrolled, involuntary, and disorganized. The third is that thought isolates us: no one can read our minds or think our thoughts for us. (Notice, by the way, that each of the reasons Steiner offers for why thought makes us sad could just as easily be cause for celebration.) At the same time, he says, as thought cuts the individual off from others, almost everything an individual thinks is banal, unoriginal, hence, the worst of both worlds. Steiner's fourth reason is that there is an inherent collision between rational demands for thought to have one truthful, verifiable meaning and the tendency of language to suggest ambiguous, evasive, multiple meanings. The fifth reason is that thought is incredibly wasteful; even Einstein claimed he had only two ideas in his entire life and the rest was dross. The sixth reason thought makes us sad is that it causes us to have fantasies and unrealistic expectations which are then frustrated or disappointed by reality. Seventh reason: we cannot arrest thought, it keeps going incessantly, like our heartbeat, veiling as much as it reveals. Eighth reason: thinking keeps us strangers from one another, prevents empathy. (I believe Steiner has started to repeat himself at this point.) Ninth reason: the enormous disparity between clever people and dull-witted ones, and the near-impossibility of teaching skills of original thinking, leads to elitism and profound social injustice. And the tenth reason, as David Letterman might say: the capacity for thought shows its limits as soon as one tries to brood over the most important questions, such as Being, Death, or God, and leads us into a glib agnosticism or a dangerous religious fundamentalism.

I'm not trying to be more demoralizing than necessary. My point is simply to suggest that in the larger culture, as well as in the specific subculture of nonfiction, we may be moving away from the complexities of thought or consciousness for understandable if ignoble reasons. If thinking on the page makes us sad, why do it? If all those semicolons, ideas, and oppositional clauses slow us down and keep us from the more tactile pleasure of sense details, speedy dialogue, and cinematically imaginable scenes, get rid of them!

I can think of another reason, which Steiner doesn't mention, for why thoughts make us sad. We may feel we know too much, or come to know it too early, which is the guilty burden of precocity. Children play to the expectations adults have of them, to behave in a childlike manner, but inside, they may not regard themselves as innocent so much as confused. I grew up sensing that a part of me was faking being a child; I felt I was already an old soul. Lots of people feel that, particularly those who will go on to become writers.

Consciousness makes us aware that we are divided, made up of disparate, contradictory parts. When children, caught in the act of misbehaving, insist "It wasn't my fault," what do they mean exactly? One part of them knows very well it was their fault, and another part believes it isn't, because it's the fault of a world so poorly constructed as to have tempted them into a wrongful act. They might want to believe they are innocent angels, as adults tell them they are, just as the adults tell them Santa Claus is real;

the trouble is they are already conscious. And guilt and shame come from consciousness, more so than from doing evil. Dostoevsky's narrator in *Notes from Underground* asserts that "consciousness is a disease." Of course the Underground Man was proud of his diseased consciousness and wouldn't have minded infecting everyone.

There remains the fear of "overthinking" a problem. How does consciousness, once it gets going, know when to stop? "I think therefore I am" becomes "As long as I'm thinking, I must still be alive." Reflecting becomes a magical way to forestall death; Poe in "The Premature Burial" dramatized that Gothic dimension of consciousness.

But if consciousness isolates, it also heals and consoles. In my own writing I am trying to say, among other things, "This is my consciousness, now don't feel so guilty about yours. If you have perverse, curmudgeonly, conflicted, antisocial thoughts, know that others have them too."

Let me speak of another misunderstanding that leads to unnecessary guilt. A graduate student who had taken a workshop with me told me she was embarrassed and perplexed about something, and could I help her out. I said I could try. She said that in her first workshop session with a new professor, he had admonished them to write from their passions, or better yet, their obsessions. I knew where the professor was coming from, having given plenty of similar pep talks, especially when I had to get through the first class hour before sending students home with the syllabus, but I also sympathized with this woman, a smart, talented personal essayist, when she confessed that she didn't think she had any obsessions, and she feared it was an indication of her shallowness.

I told her I thought obsession was overrated—in any case, far less common in real life than in fiction or movies. If by "obsession" we mean you can't think about anything else, you are an involuntary slave to an action or ideal image, I would imagine it impedes creativity. When an arty filmmaker starts shooting a film without much of a script, he gets a pretty woman to walk around the moody rain-slicked streets and then—because he knows he needs a plot—has his hero or antihero follow her. In arty films, obsession is the last desperate refuge to pull together random footage with a semblance of plot. In real life, it's not so easy to be obsessed. You say to yourself, "I think I'll stalk that person who has been on my mind," and then you decide, "Nah, I have to finish my work," or, "No, that's silly, she's not going to like me any better because I'm following her around." The practical mind kicks in. There have been times in my life when I've actually tried to promote a passionate obsession with some person or idea, because it seemed like a solution to feeling at loose ends, and in the midst of trying to obsess, I would start to giggle, as if to say, "Who am I kidding?" Maybe I'm just not the obsessive type and am therefore generalizing from too-narrow experience. But I continue to believe that obsession is more a romantic construct than an everyday occurrence.

The second problem with obsession is that it tends to go nowhere. I *have* met obsessive types in my wanderings, and mostly they were pretty boring. Obsessives repeat themselves, while ignoring other people or stories breaking around them; it's an exceedingly redundant form of thinking, so I'm not sure how useful it is in the production of nonfiction. Maybe obsession is a tool better suited for fiction; we nonfiction writers don't need it. Then what *is* needed to generate nonfiction? I would say curiosity. It may sound more tepid than obsession or passion, but it is vastly more dependable in the long run. You follow out a strand of curiosity and pretty soon you've got an interesting digression, a whole chapter, a book proposal, a book. The solution to entrapment in the narcissistic hothouse of self is not to relinquish autobiographical writing, but to expand the self by bringing one's curiosity to interface with more and more history and the present world.

Curiosity is the practical solution for the successful memoirist's second-book problem: you have to mine new material. At any rate, this was the solution I came to after having written three collections of personal essays, two volumes of personal poetry, and an autobiographical novel. I could keep cannibalizing whatever chunks of my past were still unwritten, or I could go out into the world and ruminate, that is to say, project my consciousness onto it. So I wrote a book about the New York waterfront. I read everything I could about the history, marine biology, urban planning, literature, and politics pertinent to the shoreline. I wrote about dock construction, shipworms, corrupt unions, Robert Moses and Joseph Mitchell, pirates and sailors, homeless people and public housing, and I also wrote about my own odd experiences walking the waterfront, because I found that it wasn't necessary to jettison my I-character on this journey. If anything, the voice I had developed in my personal essays was essential for welding together the disparate subjects to which my curiosity had led me. The path of my consciousness through all this obdurate technical material became the unifying element.

A confession: I was never obsessed with the waterfront. It offered a pretext and a structure for me to follow out my interests in a dozen different directions. This formula of curiosity-driven research plus personal voice is one of the most prevalent modes in today's successful nonfiction, from Rebecca Solnit to Philip Gourevitch to Jonathan Raban, from travel writing to nature writing to family chronicles to political investigations.

Not obsession but curiosity. It is my underlying conviction that nonfiction as a practice tends toward reason, calm, insight, order. This temperate, rational inclination is not such a bad thing, but we nonfiction writers sometimes feel guilty about it and want to heat up the form, make it more irrational. Much modernist literature, from Dostoevsky to Faulkner to Jim Thompson, has staked out the territory of the irrational, via the deranged, retarded, psychotic, or otherwise reason-impaired narrator. Autobiographical nonfiction has traditionally encouraged readers to regard the narrator, whatever else his flaws, as reliable, sincerely attempting to level with us. It's the difference between *Lolita* and *Speak, Memory*—between a moral monster (as Nabokov insisted in interviews his charming Humbert Humbert was) and a dependably reminiscent narrator.

I am intrigued in this regard by such autobiographical accounts as *Memoirs of My Nervous Illness* by Daniel Paul Schreber, a nineteenth-century jurist who suffered from paranoid delusions and was locked up in an insane asylum, and *The Future Lasts Forever*, by the French Marxist philosopher Louis Althusser, who strangled his wife in a moment of delirium. What moves me about these memoirs is that both authors were trying to write as rationally as possible about their brushes with madness. They were not in it for literary glory nor to flirt with a "derangement of the senses," in the Baudelaire manner, but were compelled to hold tightly to whatever shards of sanity still existed, by trying to relate the horrible experience of losing their minds. Reason can be a rare, prized, hard-to-regain commodity. So let us not disdain the classic mandate of the nonfiction writer to make sense of the world, to tell about it in lucid, rational terms.

We always come back to that strange prohibition, "Show, don't tell," which calls to mind the Clinton administration's order to gays in the military: "Don't ask, don't tell." Why this repression of the telling voice today? Traditionally, you called someone who could spin a narrative a "story*teller*." I understand some of the legitimate mistrust of telling that students voice in workshop:

they don't want the writer to do the work for them as readers; they would prefer to come to their own conclusions based on hints and suggestions. But where is it written that Jamesian indirection is the one and only valid literary method? Of course, if you're going to tell the reader directly what's on your mind, you have an obligation to make the "telling" passages as vivid and candid as possible.

Nonfiction has some relationship to the pursuit of truth—it is one of the last remaining dignities that can reasonably be deduced from its negative name. But as soon as I assert that I am writing "the truth," my palms sweat and I think I am about to perjure myself: such is the essayist's equal attachment to skepticism. "What is truth?" said Pontius Pilate, who probably wrote elegant essays in his spare time. I would be more willing to attach myself to the word "honesty." We may not ever be in possession of the truth, but at least as nonfiction writers we can try to be as honest as our courage permits. Honest to the world of facts outside ourselves, honest in reporting what we actually felt and did, and finally, honest about our own confusions and doubts. Certainly, a completely made-up fiction can achieve its own artistic honesty, but that is a separate and more speculative use of the word. The challenge faced by the nonfiction writer is to take something that actually happened, to herself or to others, and try to render it as honestly and compellingly as possible. In giving it shape, the nonfiction writer may be obliged to leave out some facts, combine incidents or even rearrange chronologies. Fine: I do not think we need apply the strictest journalistic standards of factual accuracy to all literary nonfiction. The press spends far too much time worrying these "law and order" ethical questions, probably because it is easier to pounce on discrepancies between the written and lived record than it is to fathom the formal art of personal narrative.

In my own practice, whenever possible, I would rather employ the actual facts in a nonfiction piece, because there is something magical and uncanny about the world as it is given to us, in the very randomness or order that it is given to us. Perhaps because I do keep writing fiction, I see no reason to try to make my nonfiction read like fiction. I can appreciate that the traditional attributes of nonfiction possess their own charm and validity and am not so drawn to hybridizing forms. But many today are.

A few years ago I was rushing to a doctor's appointment and I passed someone who had the *New York Post* open to a big tabloid headline, "Nonfiction Reads Like Novel," with a picture of gossip columnist Liz Smith grinning beneath it. Holy moly, I thought, everyone's getting into the act! I started to feel persecuted; there were signs and omens everywhere. It turns out Liz Smith was plugging her friend John Berendt's new book, *The City of Falling Angels*: "This tale of the glamorous, fetid, mythic, schizophrenic, slowly sinking city on the Adriatic Sea—along with its evasive denizens—makes for a hypnotic read. Berendt is the best at what he does, and what he does is persuade the reader to close his book and say, 'What a fabulous novel!' Then you realize with a start, it's all true—facts fashioned like exquisite Venetian glass." Now, I would have thought that facts fashioned like exquisite Venetian glass would be considered at least as much the province of nonfiction as fiction. Look at Edward Gibbon's magisterial synthesizing of historic details in *The Decline and Fall of the Roman Empire*, which no ever suggested read like a novel, though it *is* a magnificent story. The key distinction regarding genre merging in Liz Smith's excitable description is not about facts treated as glass, but this: "makes for a hypnotic read." It is only when you the reader are put under a hypnotic spell that you can be said to enter fictive space. That will-less absorption in another's word pictures, that abandonment of your mind to another's command seems to me the siren song of popular fiction. Obviously, not all fiction functions this way, or demands such surrender, but the "hypnotic" state, I believe, represents the desired condition when people speak about nonfiction reading like fiction.

I continue to love reading novels, and fortunately there is such a backlog of great world literature that I will never run out of worthy ones. But sometimes I find myself resisting the contrivances, the machinery of contemporary fiction. A friend of mine who is a professional novelist keeps writing personal essays on the side, not seriously, more like a holiday from fiction. Often, when I read her novels, which are always ambitious and well written, I get the feeling that the characters and situations are being mechanically coerced toward tragedy or farce. Then I pick up a personal essay by her and it's completely convincing: witty, relaxed, guided by a warmly intelligent narrative voice. The reason is probably that she didn't have to invent, she could just sculpt into words a piece of lived experience—not an easy thing to do, but since she is already a trained literary artist, she knows how to go about doing it. Sometimes imagination can be too facile, too cheap, and would benefit from a disciplined restraint put upon it.

I once heard Philip Roth deliver a talk on his latest novel, *The Plot against America*. What struck me most was this great writer saying that every night he would go to bed reminding himself, "Don't invent, remember." Sure enough, the first two-thirds of that novel are remarkable for the plausible way that everyday events come across, seeming so close to remembered fact; it's only in the last third, when the plot gets all speeded up and absurd, and Charles Lindbergh becomes the right-wing president, that the book loses its poise and turns overly gimmicky. We should not be so in awe of invention; it can be a fairly cheap knack.

We also need to recognize that some of our best recent writers were arguably better at nonfiction than fiction. Though they usually preferred to think of themselves as novelists, none of them ever created a character as vibrant as his/her nonfiction narrator, be it Mary McCarthy, George Orwell, James Baldwin, Gore Vidal, Norman Mailer ("Aquarius"), Susan Sontag, or Joan Didion. So nonfiction has nothing to apologize for. It can hold its head up high.

# On the Necessity of Turning
# Oneself into a Character

In personal essays and memoir, nothing is more commonly met than the letter *I*. I think it is a perfectly good word, one no writer should be ashamed to use. First person is especially legitimate for personal writing, so drawn to the particulars of character and voice. The problem with *I* is not that it is in bad taste (as college composition courses used to teach), but that fledgling autobiographical writers may think they've said or conveyed more than they actually have with that one syllable. In their minds, that *I* may be swimming with background and a lush, sticky past and an almost too fatal specificity, whereas the reader encountering it for the first time in a new piece sees only a slender telephone pole standing in the sentence, trying to catch a few signals to send on. In truth, even the barest *I* holds a whisper of promised engagement and can suggest a caress in the midst of more stolid language. What it doesn't do, however, is give us a clear picture of who is speaking.

To do that, the writer needs to build herself into a character. And I use the word *character* much the same way the fiction writer does. E. M. Forster, in *Aspects of the Novel*, drew a famous distinction between "flat" and "round" characters—between those fictional personages seen from the outside who acted with the predictable consistency of Dickensian caricatures, and those whose Woolfian complexities or teeming inner lives we came to know. James Wood has argued that Stephen Greenblatt's distinction between "transparent" and "opaque" characters is more helpful than Forster's. But whether the writer chooses to present characters as flat, round, transparent, opaque, or a combination of these, the people on the page—it scarcely matters whether they appear in fiction or nonfiction—will need to become knowable enough in their broad outlines to behave plausibly, and at the same time free-willed enough to intrigue us with surprises. The art of characterization comes down to establishing a pattern of habits and actions for the person you are writing about and introducing variations into the system. In this respect, building a character is a pedagogic model, because you are teaching the reader what to expect.

So how do you turn *yourself* into a character? First of all, you need to have—or acquire—some distance from yourself. If you are so panicked by any examination of your flaws that all you can do is sputter defensively when you feel yourself attacked, you are not going to get very far in the writing of personal essays. You need to be able to see yourself from the ceiling: to know, for instance, how you are coming across in social situations, and to assess accurately when you are being charming and when you seem pushy, mousy, or ridiculous. From the viewpoint of honest personal writing, it is just as unsatisfactory or distorting to underrate yourself all the time and claim you are far less effective than you actually are, than to give yourself too much credit. The point is to begin to take inventory of yourself so that you can present that self to the reader as a specific, legible character.

A good place to start is your quirks. These are the idiosyncrasies, stubborn tics, antisocial mannerisms, and so on that set you apart from the majority. There will be more than enough time later to assert your common humanity, or better yet, to let the reader make the mental bridge between your oddities and those of everyone else. But to establish credibility, you would do well to resist coming across as absolutely average. Who wants to read about that bland creature, the regular Joe? The mistake many would-be essayists and memoirists make is to try so hard to be likable and nice, to fit in, that the reader, bored, begins craving stronger stuff (at the very least, a tone of authority). Literature is not a place for conformists and organization men. The skills of the kaffeeklatsch—restraining one's expressiveness, rounding out one's edges, sparing everyone's feelings—will not work as well on the page, if your goal is to create a memorable and compelling narrator.

The irony is that most of us suspect—no, we *know*—that underneath it all we *are* common as dirt. But we may still need to maximize that pitiful set of quirks, those small differences that seem to set us apart from others, and project them theatrically, the way actors work with singularities in their physical appearance or vocal texture. In order to turn ourselves into characters, we need to *dramatize* ourselves. I don't mean inventing or adding colorful traits that aren't truly ours; I mean positioning those that are already in us under the most clearly focused, sharply defined light. It's a subtractive process: you need to cut away the inessentials and highlight just those features in your personality that most quickly characterize you, preferably those that lead to the most intense contradictions and ambivalences.

A piece of personal writing needs conflict, just as a short story does. Without conflict, your personal essay or memoir will drift into static mode, repeating your initial observation, and will come across as self-satisfied. What gives personal writing dynamism is the need to work out some problem, especially a problem that is not easily resolved. Fortunately, human beings are conflicted animals, so there is no shortage of tensions governing our lives. Experienced personal essayists know how to select a topic in advance that will generate enough spark in itself, and how to frame the topic so that it will be neither too ambitious nor too slight—so that its scale is appropriate for satisfactory exploration. If you are serenely unconflicted when you first sit down to write, you may find yourself running out of steam. If you take on a problem that is too philosophically large or historically convoluted, you may choke on the details and give up.

Still, these are technical matters, and I am inclined to think that what stands in the way of most personal writing is not technique but psychology: what's needed is the emotional preparedness and the generosity, if you will, to be honest and open to exposure.

The fledgling personal writer may be torn between two contrasting extremes:

a. "I am so weird that I could never tell on the page
   what is really secretly going on in my mind."

b. "I am so boring, nothing ever happens to me out of
   the ordinary, so who would want to read about me?"

Both extremes are rooted in shame, and both reflect a lack of worldliness. The first response ("I am so weird") exaggerates how isolated one is in those "wicked, wicked thoughts of mine," to quote Nietzsche, instead of recognizing that everyone has strange, surreal, or immoral notions. The second response ("My life is so boring and I'm so boring") requires a reeducation so that one can be brought to acknowledge just those moments in the day, in our loves and friendships, in our family dynamics, in our historical epoch, in our interactions with the natural world, that remain genuinely perplexing, vexing, uncanny, luminous, unresolved. In short, one must be nudged to recognize that life remains a mystery—even one's own so-called boring life. There must also be some recognition of the charm of ordinary daily existence, which has nourished some of the most enduring nonfiction.

The use of literary models can be a great help in invoking life's mystery. I like to remind myself, as well as my students, of the tonal extremes available: we can rant as much as Dostoevsky's Underground Man or Céline's or Bernhard's narrators, we can speak (as the poet Mayakovsky says) "At the Top of My Voice," we can be as passionate and partisan as Hazlitt or Baldwin, or even whine, the way Joan Didion sometimes does, with self-aware humor. We can try to adopt the sane, thoughtful, responsible manner of George Orwell or E. B. White. From all these models a writer of personal narrative can then choose how measured or feverish she wants to come across at any time: in one piece, she can sound like the soul of reason; in another, a step away from the loony bin.

Mining our quirks is only the beginning of turning ourselves into characters. We are distinguished one from the other as much by our past conditions, the set of circumstances in our backgrounds, as by the challenges we have encountered along the way. It means something very different to have been the second-oldest boy in an upper-middle-class Korean family that emigrated from Seoul to Los Angeles than to have been born the youngest female in a poor Southern Baptist household of nine.

Ethnicity, gender, religion, social class, geography, political affiliation: these are all strong determinants in the development of character. Sometimes they can be made too much of, as in the more limiting sort of identity politics, which seeks to explain all the intangibles of a human being's destiny by this or that social oppression. But we must be bold in working with these categories as starting points and not be afraid to meditate on our membership in each of these communities, and the degree to which it has—or has not—formed us.

When you are writing a memoir, you can set up these categories and assess their importance one by one and go on from there. When you write personal essays, you can never assume that your readers will know a thing about your background, regardless of how many times you have explained it in previous essays. So you must become deft at inserting that information swiftly—I might say, "I was born in Brooklyn, New York, of working-class parents"—and not worry about the fact that it may be redundant to your regular readers, if you're lucky enough to have any. In one essay you may make a big thing of your regional background and very little of your religious training; in another, just the opposite; but in each essay it would be a good idea to tell the reader both, simply because this sort of information will help to build you into a character.

In this sense, the personal writer must be like a journalist, who respects the obligation to get in the basic orienting facts—who, what, where, when, and why—as close to the top of every story as possible.

So now you have sketched yourself to the reader as a person of a certain age, sex, ethnic and religious background, class or region, possessing a set of quirks, foibles, strengths, and peculiarities. Are you yet a character? Maybe not: not until you have soldered your relationship with the reader by springing vividly into his mind, so that everything your I says and does on the page seems somehow oddly, piquantly characteristic. The reader must find you amusing—that's the crux of it—amusing enough to follow you, no matter what topic you propose. Whether you are writing this time about world peace or a piece of chalk, readers must sense quickly from the first paragraph that you are going to keep them engaged. The trick, of course, is that you cannot amuse the reader unless you are already self-amused. And here we come to one of the main stumbling blocks placed before effective personal writing: self-hatred.

It is an observable fact that most people don't like themselves, in spite of being decent-enough human beings—certainly not war criminals—and in spite of the many self-help books urging us to befriend and think positively about ourselves. Why this self-dislike should be so prevalent I cannot pretend to understand; all I can say, from my vantage point as a teacher and anthologist of the personal essay, is that an odor of self-disgust mars many performances in this genre and keeps many would-be personal writers from developing into full-fledged professionals. They exhibit a form of stuttering, of never being able to get past the initial, superficial self-presentation and diving into the wreck of personality with gusto.

The proper alternative to self-dislike is not being pleased with oneself—a smug complacency that comes across as equally distasteful—but being *curious* about oneself. Such self-curiosity (of which Montaigne was the fountainhead and greatest exemplar) can only grow out of that detachment or distance from oneself about which I spoke earlier. I am convinced that self-amusement is a discipline that can be learned; it can be practiced even by people such as myself, who have at times a strong self-mistrust. I may be very tired of myself in everyday life, but once I start narrating a situation or set of ideas on the page, I begin to see my I in a comic light, and I maneuver him so that he will best amuse the reader. Maintaining one's dignity should not be a paramount issue in personal writing. But first must come the urge to entertain or at least provocatively stimulate the reader. From that impulse everything else follows.

There is also considerable character dimensionality to be derived from expressing your opinions, prejudices, half-baked ideas, etc., provided you are willing to analyze the flaws in your thinking and to consider arguments against your fixations and not be too solemn about it all. Nonfiction writing thrives on daring, darting, subjective flights of thought. You must get in the habit of inviting, not censoring, the most far-fetched, mischievous notions, because even if they prove cockeyed, they may point to an element of truth that would otherwise be inaccessible.

Finally, personal nonfiction writers would do well to follow another rule of fiction writers, who tell you that if you want to reveal someone's character, actions speak louder than words. Give your protagonist, your I-character, something to do. It's fine to be privy to all of I's ruminations and cerebral nuances, but consciousness can only take us so far in the illumination of character. Particularly if you are writing a memoir piece, with chronology and narrative, it is often liberating to have the I-character step beyond the observer role and be implicated crucially in the overall action. How many memoirs suffer from a self-righteous setup: the writer telling a story in which Mr. or Ms. I is the passive recipient of the world's cruelty or is exposed to racism or betrayal, say. There is something off-putting about a nonfiction story in which the I is infinitely more sinned against than sinning. By showing our complicity in the world's stock of sorrow, we convince the reader of our reality and even gain his sympathy.

How much more complicated and believable is George Orwell's investigative left-wing self, the I in *The Road to Wigan Pier*, for having admitted he found the coal miners' smells repellent, or James Baldwin's I in *Notes of a Native Son*, for acknowledging how close he came to the edge with his rages against racism in restaurants! Character is not just a question of sensibility. There are hard choices to be made when a person is put under pressure, and it is in having made the wrong choice, curiously enough, that we are made all the more aware of our free will and humanity. So it is that remorse is often the starting point for good personal writing, whose working out brings the necessary self-forgiveness (not to mention self-amusement) that is necessary to help us outgrow shame.

I have not touched on some other requirements of good personal writing, such as the need to go beyond the self's quandaries, through research or contextualization, to bring back news of the larger world. Nor have I spoken of the grandeur of the impersonal, formal essay. Yet even when the word *I* plays no part in the language of criticism or other nonfiction, a firm sense of personality can warm the voice of the impersonal narrator. When we read a Samuel Johnson or Edmund Wilson or Lionel Trilling or Susan Sontag essay, for instance, we feel that we know these authors as fully developed characters (prickly, tolerant, combative, judicious), regardless of their not having referred personally to themselves at all in those pages.

The need thus exists to make oneself into a character, whether the nonfiction uses a first- or third-person narrative voice. I would further maintain that this process of turning oneself into a character is not self-absorbed navel gazing, but rather a potential *release* from narcissism. It means you have achieved sufficient distance to begin to see yourself in the round: a necessary precondition to transcending the ego—or at least writing personal nonfiction that can touch other people.

# Reflection and Retrospection:
# A Pedagogic Mystery Story

## 1.

In writing memoir, the trick, it seems to me, is to establish a double perspective that will allow the reader to participate vicariously in the experience as it was lived (the child's confusions and misapprehensions, say), while benefiting from the sophisticated wisdom of the author's adult self. This second perspective, which takes advantage of a more mature intelligence to interpret the past, is not merely an obligation but a privilege and an opportunity. In any autobiographical narrative, whether memoir or personal essay, the marrow often shows itself in those moments where the writer analyzes the meaning of his or her experience. The quality of thinking, the depth of insight, and the willingness to wrest as much understanding as one is humanly capable of arriving at—these are guarantees to the reader that a particular author's sensibility is trustworthy and simpatico. With me, it goes further: I have always been deeply attracted to just those passages where the writing takes an analytical, interpretative, generalizing turn: they seem to me the dessert, the reward of prose.

So it startled me when I began to discover among my writing students a fierce reluctance to allow their current, mature reflections to percolate through accounts of past experiences. When I say "writing students" I mean not only undergraduates, but graduate MFA candidates in creative nonfiction, who had dedicated themselves, at great fiscal expense and personal sacrifice, to the lifelong practice and, often, teaching of literature. Many already possessed admirable stores of technique, talent, and ability to engage the reader, and I liked them as people, so I was dismayed when I found these students resistant to the activity of retrospective thinking on the page. I had to guard against taking it personally, as a rejection of my own innermost literary sensibility, or as an omen betokening one of those generational cultural divides that plunge middle-aged professors into morose speculations that it may be time to hang it up. Since most of my students seemed disposed to learn from me, I decided to regard this particular reluctance impersonally, as a curious phenomenon that I needed to understand better.

Over the course of the semester, many of them came around to what I was pitching and developed a greater fluency in handling the double perspective. Whether the change was merely a temporary one, to please their professor, or a permanent shift, I have no way of knowing. What interests me here is not to show how some pedagogic method worked in unblocking their resistance, but to analyze the reasons for that resistance in the first place. I hope by doing so to reveal something about the current practice of creative writing instruction, as well as the changing nature of the memoir, and perhaps the difficulty of thinking itself.


My students wanted to walk the reader through their experiences as they happened or, I should say, as they relived them in memory. In the early, rough-draft stages, there are few things more pleasurable than bringing up a memory and transcribing it directly, like a wide-awake dream. Some got no further than accumulating these verbal snapshots and never did hit upon an overseeing narrative voice to provide the necessary connective glue or thematic context. But this is what they liked to do, transcribe memories as they came, without (in their words) "clogging up the narrative" with hindsight. I argued that it was not a clogging up but an essential counternarrative: that is, one strand reported on what happened, and another, equally important, speculated on the meaning of those events, through the ongoing dialectic between their prior and present intelligences. But I find it interesting in itself that they saw such commentary as merely an interruption.

This double perspective is particularly valuable in the setup, in which the memoirist would do well to tell us or at least hint at how old he or she was at the time the story begins, where the episode was taking place geographically and in what epoch, and something of the protagonist's family background, class, religion, and dominant mental state at the time. This crucial information is precisely what the fledgling memoirist or personal essayist often leaves out—ostensibly because omitting it will make the story more universal (the opposite is true: omitting it will leave the reader frustrated and disoriented). One likely reason for the omission is that the emerging nonfiction writer may not know how to insert such information gracefully, and so takes an active dislike to summaries. True, we have all encountered deadly summaries: the obligatory rehash of facts and ideas, the cursory condensation of years. The problem is not with summaries per se but with badly written ones. The student memoirist must be challenged to bring the most lively, idiosyncratic style to bear on just these summarizing, "telling" passages, so that they will sparkle with personality, brio, and active reflection.

Consistently, students who have taken many workshops, before landing in mine, will point to just the interpretative, ana-

lytical moment in a fellow student's work as the offending passage and assert that they could have intuited the same idea from
the actions and dialogue scenes. This I doubt, by the way, but
they have been taught to pounce on reflective prose as foreign
matter. Even if it were the case that they could have intuited the
same insight strictly from scenes, I still would want to encourage emerging writers to put into words what they think about an
experience when retelling it.

The nonfiction student's reluctance to provide summary and
analysis shows the markings of that nefarious taboo of writing
programs everywhere: "Show, don't tell." Leaving aside how
much this simplistic precept has validity even in fiction (consider
the strong essayistic tendency in novelists from Fielding, George
Eliot, Balzac, Tolstoy down to Proust, Mann, Musil, Kundera,
Sebald, Foster Wallace), I would argue that literary nonfiction
is surely the one arena in which it *is* permissible to "tell." In personal essays and memoirs, we must rely on the subjective voice
of the first-person narrator to guide us, and if that voice never
explains, summarizes, interprets, or provides a larger sociological
or historical context for the material, we are in big trouble. We
are reduced to groping in a dark tunnel, able to see only two feet
in front of us. (The current fashion for present tense helps writing students sustain the illusion that they are still in the dreamy
trance state that a recalled memory resembles, even as it destroys
the possibility of judging its meaning through hindsight.) Now, I
don't deny it can be exciting to grope myopically in the dark, for
a while, but any autobiographical narrative of extended length
will most likely need to vary its handling of time, by alternating
here-and-now moments with synoptic ones.

\* \* \*

The objection voiced most frequently to my urging a double perspective on memoir writers is "But I didn't know any of that then!" My students seemed to feel they would be lying, or giving themselves too much credit, if their narrators were to assert more understanding on the page than their protagonists actually possessed at that period of their lives. I quickly countered with just the sort of literary argument you might expect: that their narrator and their protagonist were two different creatures, and therefore the narrator *would* know things the I-character didn't; that all of nonfiction is an imaginative shaping of facts into a pointed narrative. No dice.

Beyond that, they seemed convinced that the "suspense" in their autobiographical narratives would be ruined if the insights in their protagonist's quest for self-knowledge were leaked to the reader too early in the game. Students love to justify vagueness in their writing by saying they don't want to give away the mystery. I tried reassuring them that there would still be no end of opportunities for suspense in the manipulation of narrative elements. They would be exchanging one mystery for another. As in any story that begins at the end (*The Death of Ivan Ilych*, say, or *Chronicle of a Death Foretold*), the reader may know what is going to happen but not how. Besides, in autobiographical nonfiction, the reader's confidence in the narrator is paramount: it is more important for the reader to be apprised of the larger facts of a case from the start, and then be led through the suspenseful unraveling of what the writer makes of these facts—more important for the reader to develop trust in a worldly, confiding, forcefully eloquent narrative voice from the start—than to be placed in the fumbling hands of a naif. The real danger was in leaving the reader with the feeling of being cheated by the writer's withholding of key information. Of course, all literary narrative involves deferring *some* information to a later point, when it will have been set up to produce maximum effect, but just as mystery writers must obey certain unspoken rules about how long to suppress evidence, so the diplomacy of the memoirist is in knowing which facts can be happily deferred and which will cause the reader to holler, "Foul!"

For example, I had a student who was writing a memoir about living with a multiple personality disorder (MPD). She claimed that because she had been diagnosed as such only in her late twenties, she did not want to "kill the suspense" by letting the reader in on the secret before that moment when it would occur chronologically to her protagonist in the narrative—roughly two hundred pages in. And so, she had planned to write a series of narrative vignettes that would show her youthful protagonist acting in bafflingly various ways, à la *The Three Faces of Eve*, and then provide the diagnostic key, aha! In this way, she hoped to put the reader through her own experience. I begged her not to do this. Should the book ever find a publisher, I argued, the marketing would give the secret away anyhow. Instead, I suggested she write an introduction that would explain straightforwardly what MPD was, admit that she had it, and then, at every step of the way, let her narrator offer as much insight as she could about the experiences she had undergone and how she regards that younger self now.

To her and the others, I issued my challenge: "I cannot wait until page two hundred for the intelligent narrator to arrive! The intelligent narrator must be present from page one onward!"

I also gave the example of the student writer who is erroneously criticized in workshop for using words that his seven- or nine-year-old protagonist wouldn't have known. This common, if primitive, misunderstanding would have it that stories or memoirs from inside a child's head should adhere to the age-appropriate

developmental vocabulary and syntax. The truth is that readers easily accept the convention of a child narrator using adult
vocabulary, even semicolons. It would be tedious indeed were we
forced to read a long story told in the 500-word vocabulary and
subject-verb-object sentence structure possessed by a seven-year-
old. What is important, in writing about childhood, is to convey
the psychological outlook you had as a child, not the limited
verbal range.


When did the protagonist figure out what she figured out, and
when is her narrator going to tell us? This became the personal
nonfiction workshop's central question. One of the workshop
students actually took the trouble to verify what I was saying: he
went to the library, pulled out a dozen highly regarded American
memoirs from Benjamin Franklin to Lucy Grealy, read the first
few pages, and found that they had all employed a double perspective, making use of intellectual hindsight. I was grateful that
he had not taken my word for it.

Some students, willing to concede my point, expressed uncertainty that they could pull it off. When you ask writing students
to keep reflecting about the meaning of the experiences they are
recounting, some look panicked: "You want me to think *on every
page*?" They gravely doubt that they can produce reflective language. Part of my job is to try to convince them that they are
already doing this. They are constantly taking the measure of the
distance between their prior and present selves.

Some of this resistance to retrospection may be rooted in past
instruction. Early on in my own writing career, I was taught to
sneer, as at something impossibly old-fashioned and Victorian,
at the locution "What I did not know then, but would learn at
a later date . . ." We were discouraged from letting our narrator

"peek ahead," since this semi-omniscient device, like the address to the reader, might bring excessive attention to the authorial apparatus and "take the reader out of the story." Postmodernism has since lessened the strictures against displaying authorial self-consciousness in a text, but remnants of that old bias against looking forward or backward persist, despite the fact that there are few mental acts in life more common than retrospection or hindsight.

Some of my students were intimidated; a double perspective looked too hard to coordinate. Granted, it may seem difficult at first to modulate on the page between one's previous and present consciousness, to direct the mental traffic of a divided self. Taking pity on my students, I reassured them that there are other ways besides reflective commentary by which they might insinuate authorial intelligence. They could also tweak the tone—for instance, by employing a large, formal vocabulary and ornate syntax while telling a story inside a child's head, or by using irony to let the reader in on the truth, even when the protagonist doesn't see it. The narrator might say, "I was outraged that my inconsiderate mama would not buy me every Barbie in the store." Thackeray employs such irony often in *Vanity Fair*, taking us into Becky Sharp's conniving mind.

They were cheered at the prospect of learning specific techniques that might enable them to circumvent thinking directly on the page, just as I was often reluctant to give them out. I likened myself to a psychotherapist waiting for a patient to commit to the painful work of self-awareness and change, without seeking shortcuts.

If students showed willingness to use indirect methods to insinuate more worldly perceptions, I still wondered why they were so reluctant to state, from their current understanding, what they made of their younger selves. They reverted to the objection that retrospection would be a falsification of their earlier capacity to understand, whereas I saw it as much more honest, because it better approximated their mental outlook now—which was, after all, their actual situation when writing. Could it be, I wondered, that they had a narcissistic attachment to that ignorant younger self, so fragile, so guileless, and wanted to protect it from the contamination of intellectual sophistication?

I tell my students literary nonfiction is one art that has no use for naïveté: there are no Grandma Moseses, no outsider primitives of the essay or memoir. Since I was in a hurry, growing up, to forfeit my innocence and achieve a disenchanted, worldly wisdom as fast as possible, I have had no trouble with this trade-off. I sense, however, that many of my students value innocence more highly than I do: they often write what are, to me, sentimental essays about wishing they were kids again, watching Saturday morning cartoons, free of adult cares and responsibilities. So my eagerness to have them develop the most adult, self-aware, intellectually ambitious voice on the page has to contend against their feeling that idealism and a sweet nature are bound up with a lack of acuity. It is as though I were asking them to be cynical, to bite the apple from the tree of knowledge. All literature professors are, to some extent, in the same boat, trying to awaken their charges from a sentimental optimism to the recognition of reality as a more tragically complex business, through the study of great texts. We become the bringers of bad news, connoisseurs of downers, and must seem sadistic in that respect.

What must be remembered, however, is that pure innocence is a fiction, as Freud showed long ago. Moreover, every person, no matter how young, is inhabited by coexisting developmental layers: nine-year-olds have moments of precocious cognition and startlingly shrewd insight into the people around them, and teenagers, when not being stereotypically adolescent, find within themselves shards of their forty-year-old mothers' weary understanding, alongside fragments of their doll-playing, six-year-old selves.

Students also argued against retrospective reflection by saying that it would take away from a piece's "vulnerability." They granted my criticism, in one case, that the writer lacked emotional clarity and was still in the resentful throes of a recent wounding experience (being jilted), but they thought this vulnerable rawness made the piece more interesting. Whatever my own classical, Apollonian predispositions are, I registered the class's sharp valuing of emotion over intellect, and their suspicion of intelligence itself as icy, soul-destroying. They seemed to consider emotional restraint automatically unhealthy: repressive, ulcer-causing. Students often want to write from and about their feelings. The problem with writing about feelings is that when you are immersed in a feeling, the context disappears and the I-character becomes generic. I tried to offer my conviction that emotion and thinking are not mutually exclusive but can coexist: passionately argued thought can have affective warmth, just as feelings can be thoughtfully and delicately parsed.

In the students' defenses of raw feeling, I also wondered to what extent they were clinging to a victim role, by shutting out the voice of adult judgment. To reflect deeply on the wounds inflicted on oneself in the past might lead to an admission of complicity in that suffering. As Kafka advised, "In the struggle between yourself and the world, you must side with the world." But the impetus for many emerging writers drawn to autobiographical narrative is the need to recite a tale of abuse. They persist in believing that they can claim the public's attention only if they speak with the authority of a victimized outsider, as regards racial prejudice, gender bias, sexual abuse, physical disability, multiple personality disorder, unloving parents, and so on. While these existential particulars might be a promising jumping-off point for the generation of material, there is still the need on the memoirist's part to create a complex, flawed I-character and a satisfyingly self-aware narrator. I counsel against constructing a narrative around one's victimization—always being in the right, more sinned against than sinning—if for no other reason than that the self-righteous protagonist becomes repellent. "But what if one really *is* a victim?" demanded an elderly woman graduate student, whose second husband was a philandering louse. I replied that "victim" is partly a subjective status: there are compacts struck between cuckold and philanderer; there are people who overcome horrendous childhoods or bad breaks to become whole, productive human beings, while others, raised in relatively serene, loving households, sometimes turn into self-pitying, psychically maimed adults. We do have some choice in what we make of our trials, both early and late.

Some of my students' resistance to retrospective analysis may have come partly from an unwillingness to relinquish their rage. Alongside technical advice, I was urging them, I suppose, to move from resentment and self-hate to self-amusement, or at least to stoical realism. Not that I have any right to rearrange their psyches in this way, or the power to do so, but being a writing teacher is never merely a matter of teaching writing. I have hopes for my charges' psychological well-being that go beyond their ability to write clarifying prose. Still, the victim narrative has deep roots in our culture, and so there was no way to lop off its head at one blow: it kept returning.

Another fashionable narrative that I found myself having to do battle with, in order to coax my students into subtler narrations, was the addiction scenario. In this case, the prepackaged insights supplied by Alcoholics Anonymous and its twelve-step program tend to supplant the impromptu, unorthodox reflections that might have arisen in the writer's mind, and to close down prematurely any skepticism and self-doubt. The memoirist under the sway of the addiction scenario keeps corralling his or her material into the twelve steps, and the narrative is forced to follow a lockstep progression from darkness to light. In the first half, the addict is shown unaware and in denial; then the addict submits to the authority of the detox group, and the truth that emerges from that leads to illumination, sobriety, and faith. However helpful AA may be in coping with this terrible illness, as a model for belletristic memoir its template proves overly rigid. "Denial" is too crude an explanation for the way the mind works, in undulating, aqueous layers of awareness and repudiation of the truth. Humankind can bear very little reality, T. S. Eliot may have famously warned us, but what scraps of reality the mind does let in seem to circulate freely with the unreality bits, rather than getting shunted off to a denial safe-deposit box.

The addict turns out to be another version of the innocent, protected from self-knowledge by the monster-substance that dominates the cerebral cortex.

But it was a writing student wanting to hold on to her *guilt* who put up the fiercest struggle against my advocacy of the double perspective. L., a graduate student whose thesis I was directing, had been writing a memoir about her year of working on a Native American reservation. When she started the year, she thought she could make a difference in the kids' lives, but the rez took it out of her, and she left convinced that it was hopeless, and felt guilty for abandoning the kids to a miserable life. After the experience was over, she started to gain some theoretical insight into how arrogant and "unconscious" she had been in her initial assumptions, how colonialist were her feelings of cultural superiority, and how much her disapproval of the adults' bad behavior on the reservation had been conditioned by her own family history of alcoholism and abandonment. Well and good. She wanted to tell the story in sequence, conveying her groping from ignorance to truth. The pages she produced were a fascinating mélange of powerful scenes and confusing, self-absorbed rants. When I pointed out that certain of her narrator's judgments about the characters (especially the men) seemed unbalanced or unfair, or that her protagonist seemed excessively clueless in too many situations, she said she *meant it that way*. She wanted the reader to get a picture of her as an unconscious Lady Bountiful. She was working toward that moment of revelation when the character's limited insight and later hindsight would come together, in the last third of the book, and there were some things she wanted the reader to realize, through the narrative pattern, that the protagonist or the narrator might never realize. I said this was tantamount to using an unreliable narrator. She was fine with that. I repeated the by-now-familiar directive that we cannot wait until page two hundred for the intelligent, worldly narrator to make an appearance. It seemed to me she was hanging her younger self out to dry, and not even allowing her narrator the dignity of clear thought, while operating on the dubious premise that the pattern alone would deliver these insights. This may be standard operating procedure for some fiction, but it is hardly common practice in memoirs, where we do need to trust that the narrator is leveling with us. I challenged her to come up with one example of a successful memoir in which the narrator was blinded but the reader got it anyway. She couldn't. All the models she had been drawing on were, interestingly enough, novels, but she continued to insist that she be allowed to "experiment" in this way. Far be it from me to squash a literary experiment; she was welcome to pursue it, but I was not enthusiastic about her chances of success.

You may feel that I was being too prescriptive, that she ought to have been applauded for attempting something so difficult; the problem was that it simply wasn't working, and as her teacher I felt obliged to point out that she was making a much harder road for herself. Beyond that, I have to admit I was shocked that someone would so cavalierly discard what to me were the strengths of the memoir form. Granted, like all literary forms it is still in the process of evolving, and many elements coexist in several forms, but with L.'s thesis, it seemed to me, we had finally reached the dividing line. There *are* a few hard differences between fiction and nonfiction, and one of them, to my way of thinking, was intentionally telling one's past experience in the voice of an unreliable, insight-stifling narrator. To do so is to write fiction.

L.'s was not the only instance of this practice. I had another thesis student, M., who wrote a personal essay about his grandfather, in which the narrator sounded smugly contemptuous of his whole family and embarrassed by them, until the last page, when he suddenly had a revelation that they were the salt of the earth and he was a creep. M. thought he was doing something very hip, very honest, by portraying himself as an asshole, but to me his suppression of any larger self-awareness until the last page was a disingenuous stunt. He was creating an unreliable narrator to make sense of his past, and by doing so he was evading the harder task of convincing us that the narrator is trying as much as possible to get to the bottom of the matter at hand.

## 2.

One of the profound changes to have affected serious writing in recent years has been the spread of fiction and poetry techniques into literary nonfiction: the "show, don't tell" requirement, the emphasis on concrete sensory detail and avoidance of abstraction, the use of recurrent imagery as symbolic motif, the taste for the present tense, even the employment of unreliable narrators. There has always been some crossover between the genres. I am not a genre purist and welcome the cross-pollination and have dialogue scenes in my own personal essays (as did Addison and Steele). But it is one thing to accept using dialogue scenes or lyrical imagery in a personal narrative, and quite another to insist that every part of that narrative be rendered in scenes or concrete sensory descriptions. A previous workshop teacher had told one of my students, "Creative nonfiction is the application of fictional devices to memory." With such narrow formulae, indifferent to nonfiction's full range of options, is it any wonder that students have started to shy away from making analytical distinctions or writing reflective commentary?

The vogue for the new American memoir has disguised the fact that that popularity has been accomplished partly through memoir's colonization by its sister genres, fiction and poetry. Consider one of the most influential memoirs of recent years, Frank McCourt's *Angela's Ashes*, which stays within the child's point of view throughout, conveying with considerable gusto, through dramatic scenes and vignettes, the hurly-burly of that upbringing, with nary a pullback to retrospection. It is only when little Frankie grows up, in the sequels *'Tis* and *Teacher Man*, that McCourt's narrator avails himself of the opportunity to reflect on his experience. Other memoirists, such as Lucy Grealy, Sarah Manguso, and Mary Karr, were trained initially as poets and tended to write in short prose-poem fragments that end in a deep-image hush.

It is probably no accident that many of the most popular, affecting contemporary American memoirs have reenacted the confusions of childhood and adolescence, offering the reader entry into the heady, liberating play space of the young person's imagination, without much attention paid to the formation of the protagonist's intellectual judgment. As such, they contrast strongly with the classic autobiographical literature of Saint Augustine, Michel de Montaigne, Jean-Jacques Rousseau, Edmund Gosse, John Stuart Mill, Alexander Herzen, Thomas De Quincey, J. R. Ackerley, Virginia Woolf, George Orwell, Richard Wright, and James Baldwin. The contemporary American model of the memoir would thus seem to be undergoing some mutation—via a muting of the adult superego. Perhaps this is overstating the case. Meanwhile, I note the continuing appearance of highly reflective, essayistic memoirs in our time by writers born elsewhere, such as V. S. Naipaul, Lorna Sage, Norman Manea, and Doris Lessing, which maintain the genre's appetite for thought.

I would not want to speculate on what larger social forces in our culture may be militating against the willingness to think on the page. I have no lofty vantage point from which to evaluate these large trends, nor any desire to play the grumpy old professor who laments that his students no longer want to read or think because television has shortened their attention spans and pop culture has turned their brains to mush. On the contrary, it seems to me that my students are often very intelligent, certainly no less so than those thirty years ago, and touchingly eager to imbibe the reading lists I throw at them. Where they do show hesitancy is in making judgments. This reluctance may have something to do with the way the word *judgmental* has come to be seen as a negative, meaning cross, close-minded, and elitist. Spiritual advisers and self-help guides instruct us not to judge our friends, colleagues, parents, siblings, and especially children, because that critical act will cut us off from empathy. Nevertheless, we continue to make judgments about the people around us all the time; it could even be argued that such judgments are a crucial first step toward empathy. But in a culture where making judgmental pronouncements is frowned upon as antisocial, the emerging writer feels pressure to keep these thoughts underground.

There is also an internalized fear of abstract thinking and generalizing, period. The initially salutary correction against abstract language (William Carlos Williams's "no ideas but in things") has gone too far, extending to a virtual gag order in students' minds against abstraction. The greater sensitivity that today's academy brings to issues of stereotyping seems to have rendered writing students preternaturally cautious, as though making any generalizations were invidious. It seems to me obviously desirable for a writing style to be able to move freely and easily from the concrete to the general and back. As for debatable generalizations, when a workshop voices exceptions to this or that generality in a fellow student's piece, I point out that we are not in a court of law. I would rather the emerging writer get into the habit of attempting sweeping generalizations, even if they prove not to be true in every instance, so long as they are true enough to stimulate thought. When Stendhal delivers a witty epigram about jealousy, or Oscar Wilde about hypocrisy, we allow for the standard deviation from the norm, meanwhile applauding their efforts to think in larger terms about human behavior. What is wit, if not the formulation of a behavior pattern in a pithy sentence? The ability to perpetrate condensed reflection is not only granted to genius; such skills can be acquired by the apprentice writer as well—first by bluffing, perhaps, but eventually by repetition, as a muscle is taught to stretch—until it becomes a reflex. All it requires is for the emerging writer to give himself or herself permission to try to think in wider terms.

The student memoirist's avoidance of retrospection must finally be seen as part of a larger reluctance to reflect in public.

Modesty, fear of failure, and dislike of the arrogance of thought all play their part. Most creative writing students have a surprisingly low estimation of their intellectual equipment (this is true even of those who write brilliant critical papers). They also refuse to believe, fundamentally, that anyone really wants to know what they think. Share their traumas and abuse stories and feelings, yes, but their thoughts, no. They are deathly afraid of exposing that their innermost thoughts may be banal. They imagine I am asking them to turn philosopher and have Big Ideas, which they already know don't rattle around in their heads. Frankly, I am not looking for Big Ideas. What I mean by thinking on the page is something more quicksilver and spontaneous: to question all that might have been transpiring inside and outside themselves at the time, and to catch the hunches, doubts, and digressive associations that dart through their brains.

When I ask my students to put more reflective passages in their autobiographical narratives, what I often get at first are pat sermons, drawn either from contemporary morality or self-help culture, which will tie their experience together with a neat diagnostic bow: "I realize now I had entered into a codependent relationship with Madge . . ." or "I saw I had intimacy issues." No, no, no, I say, that's not it! I want you to figure out something on your own, some question to which you don't already have the answer when you start. Then you can truly engage the reader in the adventure of following you, as you try to come up with deep, unexpected insights, without censoring. You must surprise yourself, and, when you do, it will make you elated and your prose elevated. What I want, in short, is honesty—honesty that will cut through the pious orthodoxies of the moment and ring true. There is nothing more exciting than to follow a live, candid mind thinking on the page, exploring uncharted waters.

In attempting any autobiographical prose, the writer knows what has happened—that is the great relief, one is given the story to begin with—but not necessarily what to make of it. It is like being handed a text in cuneiform: you have to translate, at first awkwardly, inexpertly, slowly, and uncertainly. To think on the page, retrospectively or otherwise, *is*, in the last analysis, difficult. But the writer's struggle to master that which initially may appear too hard to do, that which only the dead and the great seem to have pulled off with ease, is a moving spectacle in itself, and well worth undertaking.

# How Do You End an Essay?

## The Problem

I am often asked by students: How do I know when an essay is finished? It is a difficult question to answer in the abstract, and my first impulse is to say that it depends on each piece. But I know I am dodging the problem by resorting to a case-by-case approach, because underneath their inquiry is a larger, legitimate concern: If, as I maintain, an essay is the track of one's thoughts and is not dependent on any discernible deep structure such as the isosceles triangle epiphany in the modern short story, what's to say that it can't simply go on and on? Each thought leads to another, and then another, so how is one to know when the time has come to end an essay?

There are several ways I might go about answering such a question. The first is to examine various models, classic or contemporary, which have been deemed successful, and analyze how their endings were staged. The second is to meditate in a gassy, philosophical manner about the nature of the essay, its cultivation of doubt, the epistemological quandary we are up against, a snake chasing its tail, etc. The third would be to examine my own practice as an essayist, since I have always managed to come up with endings until now, and so, arguing backwards, I must know how to conclude these things. Right?

---

The trouble with the last proposition is that it may be something I instinctively know how to do but not how to explain to anyone else. In question-and-answer sessions with students, I often find myself comparing the awareness that it's time to wind up an essay with trying to dock a boat, hitting against the wall of a pier, and not being able to go any further. Such comfy metaphors, true as they may be to the existential experience of literary composition, ultimately manifest the sort of bad faith all too common in creative writing instruction, allowing the successful writer to hide behind the priestly prestige of the professional and leaving the wannabe writer mystified. I vow not to settle for such craven behavior here but to examine in good faith this problem of ending an essay, one way or another.

## Endlessness and Montaigne

As usual in discussions of essays, we have to go back to Montaigne. It is not just a matter of paying filial respects to the so-called father of the essay, but of trying to grapple with the awkward dilemma he bequeathed to his descendants by his own maddeningly self-perpetuating, open-ended style. The late Leonard Michaels put it best when he wrote, "The scandal of Montaigne's essays is that they have only an incidental relation to the consecutive logical argument but they are cogent nonetheless. Their shape is their sense. It is determined by the motions of his thoughts and feelings, not by a pretension to rigorously logical procedure."

What is unique about Montaigne is the great mental freedom he exhibited, which allowed him to chase his mind from subject to digression: to start off his essay "Of Coaches" talking about sneezing, then move on to seasickness, fear, riding in coaches, fancy dress and ostentatious display, liberal princes,

Roman amphitheaters, Chinese artillery, and segue into a stunning denunciation of the Europeans' treatment of natives in the conquest of Mexico, only to return in the end to coaches and royal litters. He is the Jackson Pollock of essayists, employing an all-over style that covers every inch of the composition with equal emphasis, rather than obeying the laws of literary perspective. In vain do we search for topic sentences, central themes, and an orderly development building toward conclusion. As early as his eighth essay in Book I, when he was still tentatively finding his way, Montaigne compared his mind to "a runaway horse, it gives itself a hundred times more trouble than it took for others, and gives birth to so many chimeras and fantastic monsters, one after another, without order or purpose, that in order to contemplate their ineptitude and strangeness at my pleasure, I have begun to put them in writing, hoping in time to make my mind ashamed of itself."

This passage is highly characteristic of Montaigne's amused, self-divided stance as both thinker and observer of his own unruly mental patterns. It is as though he refuses to take full responsibility for these cerebral meanderings, which he compares elsewhere, in "Of Vanity," to "some excrements of an aged mind." He is able to take both pleasure and shame in the parade of his wicked thoughts.

Because Montaigne kept amending his essays, adding in later editions those archaeological layers indicated by the superscript letters A, B, and C, he was free to change the endings. I've noticed that many of his essays have B and C additions tacked to the end, afterthoughts. Had he lived longer, undoubtedly there would have been D, E, F, and G amendments to the endings as well. All those postscripts undermine the sense of inevitability toward which the concluding movement might have built, although occasionally they nicely pull the whole thing together.

Sometimes they indicate a doubt that he has made the point sufficiently, which drives him toward further generalization, even sententiousness on occasion. For instance, in his famous one-page essay "Of a Monstrous Child," which argues for a more benign, relativistic response to so-called abnormality, the original ending reads, "I have just seen a shepherd in Médoc, thirty years old or thereabouts, who has no sign of genital parts. He has three holes by which he continually makes water. He is bearded, has desire, and likes to touch women." Montaigne added a paragraph in the final edition that drove the point home: "What we call monsters are not so to God, who sees in the immensity of his work the infinity of forms that he has comprised in it; and it is for us to believe that this figure that astonishes us is related and linked to some other figure of the same kind unknown to man. From his infinite wisdom there proceeds nothing but that is good and ordinary and regular, but we do not see its arrangement and relationship," and so on. Since Montaigne shied away from explicit expressions of religious faith and never sounded very convincing or comfortable talking about God, this more pious ending suggests either a failure of nerve or mistrust in the intelligent reader's ability to grasp his message from the abrupt, in-your-face ending of the shepherd without genitals. (That first ending is more like Gordon Lish's shock-effect edits of Raymond Carver's stories; the more gradual conclusion resembles Carver's own desire to cushion the fall.)

Montaigne's essays, as we know, grew longer and longer, until the majestic final essays in Book III. Faced with these happily uncompromising streams of association, the reader feels as though on an open boat launched onto the ocean, with no horizon line in sight. You just have to surrender to the waves of sentences that keep bumping you from one idea to another. These late essays are the antithesis of the topic-sentence/five-paragraph paper taught in freshman comp. Though organized around a topic—"On Some Verses of Virgil" is predominantly about sex; "Of Repentence," "Of Vanity," and "Of Experience" are more or less about what their titles indicate—they are likely to skitter everywhere, from the ancient world to current events, meantime conflating the personal with the historical and biological.

Montaigne is hard to teach, especially to undergraduates. If you try to emphasize structural niceties or symmetries—to analyze his essays as shaped artifacts—you are going against the grain of his own studied casualness. You can offer Montaigne to students in the hope that a few will get him, but rare is the undergraduate who can "relate," as they say, to that temperate self-acceptance of inconsistencies and flaws, which is too often misconstrued by the young as smugness. I myself could not make heads or tails of him in college and wondered why this old geezer was being foisted on us as one of the great authors. (Now that I have become an old geezer, I can "relate.") Montaigne is not suited to the extremities of adolescent confusion, like Kafka or Dostoevsky; he is for achieving equilibrium (and what teenager is interested in that middle-aged virtue?); he is opposed to the fanatical, apocalyptic, or otherworldly; he speaks for the everyday, for moderation, which he calls the "middle way," and most of all for experience, which takes a while to acquire.

Perhaps this is also why his final essay, "Of Experience," so masterfully sums up his approach to life. If he is still skeptical of his ability to harness reason, or insistent that "we must learn that we are nothing but fools," still reminding us that "both kings and philosophers defecate, and ladies too," he is also grateful to his kidney stones for teaching him the fine art of resignation. "Consider how artfully and gently the stone weans you from life and detaches you from the world," he says, and asks, "But is there anything so sweet as that sudden change, when from extreme pain, by the voiding of my stone, I come to recover as if by lightning the beautiful light of health, so free and so full, as happens in our sudden and sharpest attacks of colic?" The little habits or quirks that he confesses—how he scratches his ears, eats salt meats, sleeps covered up, loves sauces of all kinds, bites his tongue in his haste to eat—all these comic details have their place in the larger scheme of self-acceptance. Stop beating up on yourself, Montaigne says in this essay: "the most barbarous or our maladies is to despise our being." About purists or perfectionists he remarks, "They want to get out of themselves and escape from the man. That is madness: instead of changing into angels, they change into beasts; instead of raising themselves, they lower themselves. These transcendental humors frighten me."

I am arguing here that Montaigne's attraction to open-endedness or "endlessness," if you will, has a great deal to do with his seeking a balance, through the sifting of long experience and the acceptance of imperfection. Montaigne was a master of equilibrium; and equilibrium such as he advocated does not drive toward apocalypse or closure of any kind. What we now call "closure," in the therapeutic sense (to quote Ada Louise Huxtable: "closure, that solipsism that Americans use to replace grief"), would have made no sense to Montaigne. He was not a Romantic; and there was none of that Romantic impatience in him to resolve tensions and contradictions through transcendence or suicide. He chose the essay as a form to develop, in part, because it offered him a way to circumvent too-hasty resolutions.

One way to understand Montaigne's endlessly circling, quoting, associating approach is to contrast it with another powerful model of the form: the personal essay exemplified by William Hazlitt, the foremost Romantic essayist. What Hazlitt did, brilliantly, was to posit a unitary self, and to place that self in opposition to the world. Especially in his narrative essays, such as

"On Going a Journey," "The Fight," and "My First Acquaintance with Poets," Hazlitt thrust his autobiographical protagonist into action, taking him literally or figuratively on a journey until the inevitable end point, which has been predicted all along. (The fight is over, the friendship is finished, the walk completed, the prospect of love kaput.) Hazlitt's bristling, touchy I-character, who alternates between a hunger to bond with fellow creatures and a craving for solitude, stemming from that Romantic conviction that he is a Frankenstein's monster, a malcontent, too singular for polite society, crashes into the public realm, engages, embraces, rejects, or is rejected. The same dramatic plot occurs in Hazlitt's affecting if creepy *Liber Amoris*, which tells the sad tale of his unrequited infatuation with a barmaid.

Even when Hazlitt writes not a vignette-driven essay but a reflective, analytical one, such as "On the Pleasure of Hating" or "The Indian Jugglers," he stages a conflict between different perspectives and works through the distinctions in an orderly if passionate manner. Hazlitt's background was in philosophy; hence he was much more given to following a line of rigorous logical argumentation than Montaigne. He put flesh and blood on his arguments—not surprising for a writer whose highest artistic standard was "gusto," and whose artistic hero was Titian. By the end of a Hazlitt essay one feels the author has had a strenuous wrestling match between antagonistic sides of his persona and has pinned one of them to the mat.

In short, even in his analytical essays he stands starkly and dramatically before us as a unitary self. Virginia Woolf's appreciation of Hazlitt states: "As of all men he had the most intense consciousness of his own existence, since never a day passed without inflicting on him a pang of hate or of jealousy, some thrill of anger or pleasure, we cannot read him for very long without coming in contact with a singular character—ill-conditioned yet high-minded; mean yet noble; intensely egotistical yet inspired by the most genuine passion for the rights and liberties of mankind. . . . So thin is the veil of the essay as Hazlitt wore it, his very look comes before us."

Hazlitt's descendants include some of the most important essayists we have, such as George Orwell, Max Beerbohm, H. L. Mencken, Mary McCarthy, James Baldwin, and Joan Didion. Each set out to create a highly singular persona who would be able to give momentum to the flow of thoughts by means of a dramatized, thin-as-a-veil self-characterization. Montaigne let us in on many of his behavorial quirks but ultimately regarded himself as sane, ordinary, and representative of everyone; whereas Hazlitt saw himself as neurotic, unbalanced, and of a character fundamentally problematic—but unitary. I must admit that my own practice is closer to the Hazlitt essay model than to Montaigne's, though Montaigne's "endless," streaming option continues to intrigue me.

An interesting aside is that contemporary literary theory has cast into doubt the whole notion of the unitary self, positing that the inner core is in fact a fiction, and what we call a "self" may be more a collective reality, conditioned by the media and the expectations of others; that in any case, we are composed finally of language, and language is a product of what is outside us as much as what is within us. I have long held the personal essay to be one of the last bastions of the orthodoxy of the unitary self: those of us who are drawn to practicing this form tend to believe in our possessing a core reality or self, and we would cling to this conviction even if critical theory disproved it beyond doubt. The lyrical essay, which has recently come in vogue, offers a compromise bridge between the two notions, which allows for more of a porous, diffuse, destabilized, collective self than the individualized, Romantic essay model. Seen in this light, our progenitor Montaigne is more "modern" than Hazlitt, because he channels the wisdom of the ancients and Erasmus as though they were occupying as much space in his cerebral cortex as himself; his mind floats on an undulating current of inconstant thoughts, which his ego is paralyzed to control; and even while enumerating each little habit of his, he conveys the sense of having a permeable membrane coterminous with everyone else's: "Each man bears the entire form of man's estate." This is not merely a humanistic statement but a recognition of our shared genetic material, which dilutes the privilege of the unitary self and promotes a model of interdependence.

Endlessness has long been a literary modernist trope. Curiously, it is more often found in modern fiction than in the modern essay, though it is usually novelists of an essayistic bent, such as Proust, Musil, Bernhard, Sebald, Saramago, Marías, and Bolaño, who are given to open-ended discourse and long unbroken paragraphs that offer no end in sight. Tracing the method of novelistic endlessness back to its source, we find *Don Quixote* and *Tristram Shandy*. Sterne especially championed the practice of inexhaustible digression. Is endlessness, then, perforce comic? Certainly there is something funny about a speech never coming to an end or a narrator never coming to the point, and to the degree that death is avoided by such outtalking, the tragic is circumvented too. The Marquis de Sade, no tragedian himself, is also endless, though comic in only an inadvertent way: it is hard to know which is more horrifically absurd, the sadistic acts he describes with relish or his torturers' interminably self-justifying speeches.

Perhaps this is the moment to consider that our Western model of the shaped literary artifact, smooth as a Brancusi egg and tapering to an exquisitely polished point, may actually be quite recent and provincial. Much of the world's great literature—the Mahabharata, the Icelandic sagas, the chivalric romances such as d'Urfé's *L'Astrée, Don Quixote, The Thousand and One Nights, Gargantua and Pantagruel,* the picaresque novel, *Les Misérables, War and Peace,* Proust, and so on—has followed an open-ended, additive model, with episodic strings of adventures and complications trumping the expectation of a singular finale. Poe may have said that a poem must be short or face the risk of mounting imperfection, but *pace* Poe, perfection is very rare in literature and probably overrated. Taking the long, global view, Montaigne's practice of endless essay spinning may therefore be less of a scandal than it would at first appear.

## Getting In and Out of Jams

Most great essays are not flawless, and their endings attempt to finesse this fact. Still, literature students are encouraged to approach the canon as though everything included in it were perfect, more or less, and it is their job to figure out how the parts fit together—a mistaken assumption, which nonetheless can yield useful insights. Certainly there are great essays that are perfect, such as E. B. White's "Once More to the Lake." Every word, every comma prepares us for the thrilling last line about White and his son: "Languidly, and with no thought of going in, I watched him, his hard little body, skinny and bare, saw him wince slightly as he pulled up around his vitals the small, soggy, icy garment. As he buckled the swollen belt, suddenly my groin felt the chill of death." It's always good strategy to invoke death at the end of a literary piece, and E. B. White's control of diction (*vitals, soggy, groin*) is astonishingly apt. I have to say that as a practicing essayist I hold White's perfection against him. Maybe it's envy, because I could never control an essay's overall texture as totally, but I would much prefer to read a long rambling essay that meanders juicily into open-ended imperfection, such as Woolf's *A Room of One's Own*, than an essay by White that is mitered and joined to a tee. That skill, it seems to me, belongs more to the short story than the essay, and I can't forgive White for raising the form's standards so grievously. Then again, he did write a number of amiably flawed essays, and to be fair, Woolf wrote a perfect essay herself, "The Death of a Moth," and I have forgiven her for it. It ends with those magnificent last two lines: "The moth having righted himself now lay most decently and uncomplainingly composed, O yes, he seemed to say, death is stronger than I am."

Often the heightened ending of a great essay will attempt to distract the reader from the flaws that preceded it. "Such, Such Were the Joys . . ." by George Orwell is one of my favorite essays. It proceeds for most of its length in linear narrative fashion, recounting the grim experience the author had when he was a lad in an English boarding school. At every step of the way the adult author questions or qualifies the impressions of the credulous, ignorant boy he was, but for all that, it is an engrossing adventure story, like those classic children's books about lost, abandoned children deposited in the monster's castle or some other hostile environment. The vigor of the opening two-thirds is driven by this gothic fairytale energy. But Orwell was determined to show how he was a slave to power—how he had internalized the class prejudices of the school—and once he had done that, and realized in retrospect that the headmaster and his wife were not ogres but pitiful lost young people themselves, he seemed not to know how to go on. The narrative part of "Such, Such Were the Joys . . ." doesn't so much conclude as run out of steam. It was only after I had been teaching the essay for ten years that I realized a part of me always expected the story to go on like a Dickens novel, *David Copperfield* or *Oliver Twist*. What kept me from being disappointed was the sudden turn Orwell gave the essay, dropping the narrative mode for some fascinating candid reflections on the nature of childhood and the relations between children and adults in our seemingly enlightened present day. Orwell, the political progressive, was asking, in effect, whether, even after we have eliminated the gross inequities of society, a portion of irremediable sorrow would still fall to children. (The sorrow of adulthood is encapsulated in a last line that sounds much like Hazlitt: "How small everything has grown, and how terrible is the deterioration in myself!") This shifting of gears proved to be a very satisfying way of interrogating analytically the preceding narrative. It also successfully hid the fact that there was something structurally incomplete in the tale. You might say that the novelist in Orwell, never his most accomplished side, yielded ground to the essayist, the more commanding Orwellian persona.

Another superb writer to have practiced both forms, bringing remarkable narrative power to his personal essays (more so than to his novels), was James Baldwin. There is perhaps no greater essay in modern American literature than "Notes of a Native Son," that exploration of the tensions between Jimmy and his father, and between black and white society. Baldwin moves effortlessly between narrative, character portrait, and analysis, juxtaposing numerous time frames in the process, for twenty thrilling pages. You wonder how he is going to resolve all the harsh emotional ambivalence he has introduced. Then he gives us this final paragraph:

> It began to seem that one would have to hold in the mind forever two ideas which seemed to be in opposition. The first idea was acceptance, the acceptance, totally without rancor, of life as it is, and men as they are: in the light of this idea, it goes without saying that injustice is

a commonplace. But this did not mean that one could be complacent, for the second idea was of equal power: that one must never, in one's own life, accept these injustices as commonplace but must fight them with all one's strength. This fight begins, however, in the heart and it now had been laid to my charge to keep my own heart free of hatred and despair. This intimation made my heart heavy and, now that my father was irrecoverable, I wished that he had been beside me so that I could have searched his face for the answers which only the future would give me now.

This eloquent, elegant solution does many things at once. The idea of two clashing ideas held suspended in the mind acknowledges the reader's hunger for resolution, without giving in to false simplicities. It is of course not new, recalling as it does Keats's epistolary remarks on negative capability, or F. Scott Fitzgerald's postulate in his essay "The Crack-Up" ("The test of a first-rate intelligence is the ability to hold two opposed ideas in the mind at the same time, and still retain the ability to function"). But the specific terms assigned to the split (the wisdom of acceptance versus the unwillingness to stomach injustice) have a certain moral grandeur. Baldwin's sentences move adroitly from the general (the formal pronoun "one") to the personal "I"; the word "fight" implies summoning of aggression, a suggestion immediately belied by the injunction to free the heart of hatred; and the piece ends with a poignant, complex image of an impossibility: searching the face of someone who is no longer there, and simultaneously looking Janus-faced toward the past and future.

This ending is written in such a way that it perfectly illustrates the tortured reconciliation Baldwin feels called upon ("it now had been laid to my charge" is his curious locution) to achieve. But I also think it works so well because the essay is relatively short. Problems of scale mar Baldwin's essays once they start growing longer and longer. The more his essays became attenuated, the more unrealistic were the expectations placed on his endings to deliver a last, unifying impression.

Then again, he was not alone in struggling with endings. George Eliot admitted that "conclusions are the weak points of most authors," noting that "some of the fault lies in the very nature of a conclusion, which is at best a negation." Frank Kermode, who so formidably discussed the terminations of novels and poems in *The Sense of an Ending*, strikingly omitted to say anything about the problem of concluding essays, although he wrote nothing but, and presumably understood best, this type of composition. So we will have to soldier on as we best can, without the benefit of his wisdom.

## A Brief Typology of Endings

Is this the promis'd end?
—Kent, *King Lear*

An essay may end in an image, an epigram, a line of dialogue, a joke, a question, a quote, an ellipsis . . . In short, as many literary techniques as exist, that is as many ways as are available to conclude an essay. The ending may recapitulate some phrase introduced earlier, like the return of a refrain, or it may tweak that previous notion and transform it, give it a different spin. One way to end an essay, of which I am particularly fond, is to introduce a new insight, that has been either held in reserve just for that occasion or stumbled upon in concluding. Something fresh, in any case. An essay may end in a sudden ratcheting up of rhetorical eloquence, like Baldwin's "Notes of a Native Son," as well as in a moral summing-up, like the last paragraph Montaigne gave to "Of a Monstrous Child." Or it may peter out, not so much because the subject is exhausted as because the writer can no longer sustain the essayist persona, that high-wire act of thinking in public, balanced improbably between passion and detachment, formal and informal tones. An essay may end in a sigh, a shrug, a sudden mood change.

A common mistake students make is to assume they need to tie up with a big bow the preceding matter via a grand statement of what it all means, or what the life lesson to be drawn from it is: too often the result is a platitude. If the essayist *can* produce a nonplatitudinous larger meaning at the end, fine; if not, then an adequate ending may be achieved by adding a few more pages, it almost doesn't matter what, just so long as the illusion is sustained that the narrative arc has been completed, which may be nothing more than the reader's sense that the author has grappled as honestly, bravely, and variously as possible with the problems introduced. Some quandaries may ultimately be impossible to resolve in human terms (ambivalence toward a parent, say, or peace in the Middle East) but may still invite aesthetic resolution: that is, the reader has the sense of having been given a full mental meal and can walk away from the table satisfied.

Often the initial setup or opening sentence will forecast the ending. In an excellent paper entitled "The Endings of Essays," my student Marilyn Zion gave the example of Cynthia Ozick's "A Drugstore in Winter": "Ozick opens the essay with a statement that operates like a road map or a program at a musical event: 'This is about reading; a drugstore in winter; the gold leaf on the dome of the Boston State House; also loss, panic and dread.' By beginning with this statement, Ozick not only familiarizes the reader with the places where the essay will travel, she also piques the reader's curiosity. What do these things have in common? the reader wants to know. . . . As the short essay comes to a close, the narrator, now elderly, grows less certain and self-assured than the former youthful persona we met in the opening paragraph. The narrator, who started out making explicit statements about tangible objects, concludes the essay by asking questions about abstract concepts such as loss, panic and dread. Ozick ends with the following question, 'Your hair is whitening, you are a well of tears, what you meant to do (beauty and justice) you have not done, papa and mama are under the earth, you live in panic and dread, the future shrinks and darkens, stories are only vapor, your inmost craving is for nothing but an old scarred pen, and what, God knows, is that?'"

Ozick's movement from certainty to doubt is appropriate to essays in general, as their explorations come to honor the original question of their founder, Montaigne: "What do I know?" Among other things, an essay is a quasi-scientific experiment to discern the limits of one's knowledge. A person's thoughts may have no natural stopping point (until death, and maybe beyond that, who knows?), but a person's knowledge certainly has its limitations.

Here are other examples of aforementioned ending options, plucked from Zion's paper or at random. An essay may end in an image, such as Gretel Ehrlich's "The Solace of Open Spaces": "We fill our space as if it were a pie shell, with things whose opacity obstructs our ability to see what is already there." Or a joke: Chesterton realizing that while searching for some chalk to draw with, he is actually sitting on one giant piece of chalk. Or a sudden change of mood, such as Didion's essay on migraines, "In Bed," which, after detailing all the wretchedness of that state, concludes: "For when the pain recedes, ten or twelve hours later, everything goes with it, all the hidden resentments, all the vain anxieties. The migraine has acted as a circuit breaker, and the fuses have emerged intact. There is a pleasant convalescent euphoria. I open the windows and feel the air, eat gratefully, sleep well. I notice the particular nature of a flower in a glass on the stair landing. I count my blessings." (We are reminded of Montaigne voiding his kidney stones.) Charles Lamb's "New Year's Eve," which starts lightly then becomes a meditation on death, alters course again near the end by concluding with a jolly song and a toast. Edward Hoagland's "The Courage of Turtles" ends with a startlingly frank shrug, after he has deposited his turtle in the Hudson River and realized it was about to drown: "But since, short of diving in after him, there was nothing I could do, I walked away."

One of the loveliest endings to an essay I know can be found in Natalia Ginzburg's "He and I." After a series of short sentences that describes the way the author's husband's eccentricities differ from her own (the piece is essentially a list, which format raises perennial problems of how to conclude gracefully), she abandons the "he"/"I" seesaw structure for a longer sentence that takes us back to the days before their courtship, when everything was still up for grabs:

> If I remind him of that walk along the *Via Nazionale*, he says he remembers it, but I know he is lying and that he remembers nothing; and I sometimes ask myself if it was us, these two people, almost twenty years ago on the *Via Nazionale*, two people who conversed so politely, so urbanely, as the sun was setting; who chatted a little about everything perhaps and about nothing; two friends talking, two young intellectuals out for a walk; so young, so educated, so uninvolved, so ready to judge one another with kind impartiality; so ready to say goodbye to one another for ever, as the sun set, at the corner of the street.

By altering the syntax with a run of leisurely semicolons, Ginzburg achieves the equivalent of an overhead shot at the end of the movie, the camera pulling back to convey nostalgia, regret, perspective, ironic wisdom, and the invisible workings of destiny.


Formal analysis of the essay is still at a primitive stage in literary criticism, compared to poetry or fiction. That may not be entirely a bad thing. It means that the essayist may feel freer to chart a different course each time, without the narratological self-consciousness of deep structures, predictable forks in the road, and traditional alternatives. That is, one may still be able to fool oneself into thinking that one is launching into the unknown, and stumbling on an original shape for each essay, simply by following one's thoughts. The excitement that Montaigne felt when he realized he was doing something unprecedented by studying the universe of his own mind is available to the contemporary essayist to recover, however fleetingly. Yet that still leaves the problem: how to bring the damn thing to a close?

So far in my own experience, writing the ending of an essay has something to do with internalizing the audience's threshold of patience. If I sense the reader tapping her foot, I know I must wind up this deal. Though mindful of Montaigne's conviction that everything is connected to everything else, which would encourage any essay to open out fanlike to a thousand different associations, I realize we live in times where there are many more entertainment options than the page.

Word limits, assigned by magazine editors or instructors, are a wondrous spur to conclude. But even when none has been set, I usually start with an apprehension of scale that tells me a certain subject only merits x number of pages (bow ties, say, should get two, not ten), and to go beyond that point, however much fun one is having, risks bloat.

For me, an ending may arise from a combination of fatigue and optimism. Say I am getting tired of working on a particular essay, which I had thought would take only a day and is now stretching into its second or third week; meanwhile the material, the flattened clay or beaten metal (we are back to those metaphors again, the boat banging into the dock), is thinning under my hands. At the same time, I see a possible solution, an intriguing glimmer in the distance that could, optimistically, function as an ending. The fact that it does not resolve the problems the piece has raised but, instead, slips out of their grasp, makes a wacky diagonal run away from them, may be all to the good. Readers should be left with some things to work out on their own. I have a liberating elation of having pulled off a fast one. The next day, in a more responsible, less optimistic mood, I see that there is much more left to say. So I tinker by adding a few lines, a paragraph, and then, eventually, leave it alone. I am not interested after all in perfection; this ending will serve, it is good enough, it will have to do.

# The Uses of Contrariety

Let's begin with the assumption that the essay feasts on doubt, self-doubt, ambivalence, contradiction, and paradox. It's no accident that Montaigne, the fountainhead of the modern essay, put such emphasis on his own changeableness. In his "On the Inconsistency of Our Actions," he wrote, "All contradictions may be found in me by some twist and in some fashion. Bashful, insolent, chaste, lascivious, talkative, taciturn, tough, delicate, clever, stupid, surly, affable, lying, truthful; learned, ignorant; liberal, miserly, and prodigal: all this I see in myself to some extent depending on how I turn; and whoever studies himself really attentively finds in himself, yes, even in his judgment, this gyration and this discord. I have nothing to say about myself absolutely, simply, and solidly, without confusion and without mixture, or in one word."

Since essays require more than one word, this multiplicity and fragmentation of self comes in handy. I would add into the mix another important concept, to me at least: *resistance*. Often, I am no sooner asked by an editor to write on a certain topic than I begin to experience a nauseated opposition to the assignment. It could be laziness, or a knee-jerk reaction against authority, or it could be reluctance to comply with what I sense is a conventional exercise. So, for instance, when I agreed to contribute to an anthology of essays by Jewish-American authors about their personal relationship to the Holocaust, I ended up writing a piece called "Resistance to the Holocaust," in which I interrogated my own aversion to this subject matter. When asked to contribute to an anthology about literary mentorship, in which each author was expected to express gratitude toward an inspirational figure, I realized I had never had a mentor, properly speaking, and wrote a piece called "Terror of Mentors." In any case, I often take my own foot-dragging regarding some writing project and try to understand it and turn it into a point of entry, just as a psychoanalyst will seize on a patient's resistance to therapy in order to effectuate a breakthrough.

Nowhere is this "thinking against oneself" process, this resistance to conventional truths, more striking than in essays written in opposition to a seemingly unchallengeable good. Some examples of that tradition include Joyce Carol Oates's "Against Nature," Susan Sontag's "Against Interpretation," Witold Gombrowicz's "Against Poets," Laura Kipnis's *Against Love*, and my own "Against Joie de Vivre." Now why would one want to take such a perverse position, which flies in the face of all accepted wisdom? What is to be gained by such contrarianism?

Let me enumerate the advantages: the first is surprise, freshness, the lure of the unexpected. To write a panegyric to love, peace, or brotherhood would be to invite yawns of agreement. For an essayist to strike a mischievous pose, sometimes all that is necessary is to question skeptically a received truth. If this were done only for provocation's sake, it might aggravate or pall, but if in the process of the writer's analyzing his or her resistance some grain of truth were uncovered, it would complicate our understanding of the good in useful ways and bring solace to readers who might otherwise feel alone in their wayward, anti-social thoughts. (I suspect we all have them.) And if, in the end, the writer's attack on an ostensible positive fails to convince us, all the more strengthened will be our attachment to that particular good, having withstood the trial of devil's advocacy. In testing the validity of certain pieties, the contrarian essay performs a valuable function, like the null hypothesis in experimental science.

A second advantage is that the contrarian gambit introduces tension and suspense into the essay: how will the writer justify this absurd (it would appear on first hearing) contention? The "against" strategy is a gauntlet thrown down not only to the reader but to the writer as well, who must now come up with convincing arguments, or at least entertaining rants.

A third advantage is that a curmudgeonly pose helps to make the narrator, or I-character, come alive as a specific, idiosyncratic individual. To say you like to take walks in nature hardly distinguishes you from several billion others. To assert, as Max Beerbohm does in his funny personal essay "Going Out for a Walk," that he resists such practices at all costs is to have his "Max" spring vividly to mind. "It is a fact that not once in all my life have I gone out for a walk," he writes. "I have been taken out for walks; but that is another matter. Even while I trotted prattling by my nurse's side I regretted the good old days when I had, and wasn't, a perambulator." The wordplay on "perambulator" suggests another advantage of the contrarian essay: it is an invitation to wittiness. Earnest piety has been abandoned at the title alone, so one may as well play the sardonic, disenchanted wag. Just as wit often relies on unexpected inversion, such as in Oscar Wilde's remark that no one could read of the death of Little Nell without bursting into laughter, so the contrarian essay is an exercise in inside-out thinking.

Does it not also have a potential downside, inviting aggressiveness, bullying, and hostility toward the reader who, as society's surrogate, most likely believes in the conventional good under attack? Yes, perhaps. The trick, for the contrarian essayist, is to provoke without insulting—to alternate between cheekiness toward and bonding with the reader. This requires not only supreme control of the ironic tone but also an ability to be self-mocking at the same time as tweaking others' assumptions.

It is also useful to anticipate readers' objections. So Gombrowicz, in the first paragraph of his diatribe against poetry:

> It would be more subtle of me if I did not disrupt one of the rare ceremonies which we have left. Even though we have come to doubt practically everything, we still venerate the cult of Poetry and Poets and this is the only deity which we are not ashamed to worship with great pomp, deep bows, and inflated voice. . . . Ah, ah, Shelley! Ah, ah, Slowacki! Ah, the word of the Poet, the mission of the Poet, and the soul of the Poet! Nevertheless, I have to attack these prayers and spoil this ritual as much as I can simply in the name of elementary anger, which all errors of style, all distortions, all flights from reality arouse in us. Because I am setting out to do battle with an area especially elevated, almost celestial, I have to watch so that I don't float off like a balloon and lose the ground beneath my feet.

He then goes on to puncture the self-satisfied aura surrounding the genre in astute ways, even for those of us who love poetry.

Laura Kipnis begins her book *Against Love* with what she calls a "Reader's Advisory," like a warning label on a medicine bottle:

Please fasten your seatbelts: we are about to encounter contradictions. The subject is love, and things may get bumpy.

To begin with, who would dream of being against love? No one. Love is, as everyone knows, a mysterious and all-controlling force, with vast power over our thoughts and life decisions. Love is boss, and a demanding one too: it demands our loyalty. We, in turn, freely comply—or as freely as the average subject in thrall to an all-powerful master, as freely as indentured servants. It's a new form of mass conscription: meaning it's out of the question to be summoned by love, issued your marching orders, and then decline to pledge body and being to the cause.

By comparing love to a boss, a feudal lord, and an army bureaucracy, Kipnis tries to enlist the reader in a sort of class warfare against what she perceives as the oppressor.

When I set myself, improbably enough, against joie de vivre, the joy of life, I also included a caveat early on:

A warning: since I myself have a large store of nervous discontent (some would say hostility), I am apt to be harsh in my secret judgments of others, seeing them as defective because they are not enough like me. From moment to moment, the person I am with often seems too shrill, too bland, too something-or-other to allow my own expansiveness to swing into stage center. "Feeling no need to drink, you will promptly despise a drunkard" (Kenneth Burke). So it goes with me, which is why I am not a literary critic. I have no faith that my discriminations in taste are anything but the picky awareness of what will keep me stimulated, based on the peculiar family and class distinctions that formed me. But the knowledge that my discriminations are skewed and not always universally desirable doesn't stop me in the least from making them, just as one never gives up a negative first impression, no matter how many times it is contradicted.

So I attempted to arm the reader against my onslaught on normal pleasure.

The more difficult trick may be to navigate the line between telling the truth and being so caught up in contention as to risk disingenuousness. Some exaggeration for comic effect is of course permissible, as well as some suppression of one's more conventional tendencies for the sake of argument. When I wrote "Against Joie de Vivre," for instance, I was perfectly well aware that another side of me is much more life-affirming, and that I can on occasion enjoy a picnic or dinner party as well as the next man, just as Beerbohm, for all we know, may have liked taking occasional walks in nature. But there is something to be said for following out an impulse as far as it will take you and seeing where it will lead. Susan Sontag put it this way, justifying her quixotic stances against metaphorical and interpretative thinking: "Of course, one cannot think without metaphors. But that doesn't mean there aren't some metaphors we might as well abstain from. As, of course, all thinking is interpretation. But that does not mean it isn't sometimes correct to be 'against' interpretation."

Oscar Wilde wrote, "A truth in art is that whose contradiction is also true." It's a comforting thought, especially for those who might be inclined to worry overmuch about the distinction between truth and lies in nonfiction.

I like the way Joyce Carol Oates begins her essay "Against Nature":

*The writer's resistance to Nature.*

It has no sense of humor: in its beauty, as in its ugliness, or its neutrality, there is no laughter.

It lacks a moral purpose.

It lacks a satiric dimension, registers no irony.

Its pleasures lack resonance, being accidental; its horrors, even when premeditated, are equally perfunctory, "red in tooth and claw," et cetera.

It lacks a symbolic subtext—excepting that provided by man.

It has no (verbal) language.

It has no interest in ours.

It inspires a painfully limited sense of responses in "nature-writers"—REVERENCE, AWE, PIETY, MYSTICAL ONENESS.

It eludes us even as it prepares to swallow us up, books and all.

Oates's tone is tentative, speculative, suggestive, note-taking. It leaves an out for the lover of nature to disagree with her without feeling humiliated.

The contrarian essay often engages the reader in a bracing polemic. Here's Kipnis again: "Polemics exist to poke holes in cultural pieties and turn received wisdom on its head, even about sacrosanct subjects like love. A polemic is designed to be the prose equivalent of a small explosive device placed under your La-Z-Boy lounger. It won't injure you (well, not severely); it's just supposed to shake things up and rattle a few convictions."

In a sense, the contrarian essayist, by presenting himself or herself from the start as an oddball, allows the reader a space to entertain forbidden or antisocial thoughts with minimal risk. The reader is not being conscripted in an army of oppositionists but merely put on the alert that contrarian, heretical ways of thinking do exist.

Mary McCarthy titled her first essay collection *On the Contrary*, no doubt playing on the nursery rhyme, "Mary, Mary, quite contrary," but also setting herself up as a feisty curmudgeon who liked a good argument. H. L. Mencken gave six of his essay series the same title, *Prejudices*, so partial was he to this term, which, even in his day, held negative connotations. Part of the contrarian essayist's self-appointed task is to rescue a word that has fallen under a disapproving shadow and turn it to a more positive light. In our own time, *judgmental, discrimination, prejudice* are all words held in bad odor. But any writer who would cultivate an independent mind must first be open to receive such counterintuitive filaments of feeling and thought, such prickly distinctions.

# Imagination Thin and Thick

In these innovative if confusing times, when talk of hybrid forms and genre blending abounds, the temptation is for nonfiction writers to make their work sound as novelistic as possible. Since fiction still enjoys greater literary distinction than nonfiction, that temptation is even more understandable. However, I would caution against borrowing one particular technique from fiction writing: to imagine on the page a scene unfolding, moment by moment, that one did not oneself witness. If I am dubious about this practice, it is for two reasons.

The first, more commonly voiced objection is that it will raise the suspicions and doubts of literalist nonfiction readers, who are legitimately entitled to wonder, "How did he/she know that?" Still, I can envision a day, not too far off, when such infractions against traditional nonfiction practice come to be accepted (however regrettably) as prosaic license. The second objection, less frequently articulated, is that it is so rarely done well. The results are usually imagined perfunctorily, below the standards of a first-rate piece of fiction.

To give an example: My nonfiction graduate students are often drawn to writing about the lives of their grandparents, perhaps from a desire to grasp their own wellsprings of character, or from a sort of ancestor worship—a reverent sympathy for the sufferings and privations of their elders. So they might imagine their grandparents' hard lives in the Old Country and the passage to America and the difficult adaptations that ensued. The problem is that my students usually don't know that much about their grandparents' lives, so they have to finesse the details with a combination of imaginative speculation and research. A dictionary may give them the words for "spatula" or "hoe" in Danish, which they will gladly insert where necessary. But the effort to bring these stories alive is often doomed by a pious idealizing of their grandparents—an unwillingness to expose their elders' mixed motives, contradictions, and flaws, the way a skillful fiction writer would. Even when a saccharine fable-like approach can be avoided, the results are usually wooden and unconvincing. One has only to compare these hybridized attempts to robust fictions such as O. E. Rolvaag's *Giants in the Earth* and Willa Cather's *My Ántonia*, or Jan Troell's epic films *The Emigrants* and *The New Land*, to see how much specificity and drama is missing. They are, in a word, *thinly* imagined.

I did have one graduate nonfiction student who managed to find out enough of what happened to her grandparents, through interviews and library research, to write a compelling narrative about their escape from Nazi Germany and their subsequent treks as displaced persons. It was a vivid, suspenseful, truthful account, but she still insisted on putting in invented details, such as that someone blinked in the hot sun or looked down at his shoe instead of replying or gulped several times when drinking from a ladle. These banal portmanteau descriptions did not measure up to the factual vivacity of the rest, and I advised her to take them out, though she ignored me and chose to hold on to them.

Other examples may be gleaned from the increasingly popular practice known as "immersion reporting." A journalist with literary ambitions, say, is writing a book-length project about true crime or the lives of the rural poor. He has hung out with his subjects at length, and now he writes a scene about an unemployed construction worker sitting on a porch, talking to the sheriff, who has come by to inquire about this man's iffy nephew. The author sees in his mind's eye the unemployed man rocking back and forth, and he puts that detail in, then he sees the man scratching his nose and puts that in, or clearing his throat. ("He cleared his throat, but there was still a residue of phlegm.") All these details are the equivalent of what screenwriters call "beats"; they're facile placeholders, conventional enough, but the question is, Are they truly necessary? Do they bring us insight into this specific character, or are they so common (who does *not* scratch his nose?) as to tell us little except that the writer is trying to get a purchase on the moment until something better comes along. Moreover, these beats seem to come from the stylistic universe of popular middlebrow fiction. A detail like "He scratched his nose" is inserted ostensibly to make the scene come alive, but does it? Doesn't it, rather, intrude a further veil of *concretized abstraction*? (That may sound like a logical contradiction: what I mean is that excessive faith in sensory details can take us further away from the heart of the matter, especially if they seem pasted on instead of organically rising from the characters and the scene. A detail that pinned down, say, the precise appearance or individual psychology of a character would be far less generic.)

A student of mine was writing a superb book-length work of immersion reporting: she had spent years in the company of ex–gang members in Los Angeles who kept being thrown back in jail for violation of parole, devastating their struggling families. Something compelled her to muck up the beginning of the book

with an imagined scene of her protagonist, Luis, in jail await-
ing his release. In addition to the description of the cell, which
the author might plausibly have learned from her source or elsewhere, the reader was treated to such passages as "Luis watched
irritably as a fly buzzed through the cell's grimy, single-paned
window" or "Most of last night he felt as if tiny firecrackers were
lighting and relighting themselves right under his sternum." Now,
the fly I could live without, because it doesn't individuate Luis
as a character to know that he disliked pesky insects, but this
firecracker under the sternum seemed to me especially presump-
tuous: the reporter, an otherwise highly reliable witness, was
crawling right into the poor man's skin, or pretending to, and
had no business being there. She had every right to describe his
routine of push-ups in the cell, because that was externally, objectively verifiable, but dramatizing his dilemma with fireworks in
his sternum remains a piece of self-indulgent somatic speculation.
(She took it out.)

Had she not, some readers would have been quick to ask
that nagging question, "How did she know? Was she there in
the cell when he woke up? Obviously not." The writer who put
in the nose-scratching detail might have responded, "Look, I
spent hours with that guy and I saw him scratch his nose more
than once." Fine, but that doesn't change the way the detail was
applied, as mechanical colorization. Even more problematic is
when the nonfiction author takes us into the subjects' minds.
Remember the justifiable flak Edmund Morris received when he
wrote a biography of Ronald Reagan that included an interior
monologue of young Ron sitting on a park bench.

It's not that difficult to invent (i.e., picture in the mind's eye)
shallow scenes and glibly play out possible interior monologues
in your head: the fact that you can imagine something clearly
doesn't make it validly literary. The harder imaginative task for

nonfiction writers is that of seeing the pattern in actual experience and putting it into some order, so that what had seemed random is given narrative significance and symbolic resonance. Understanding is thick imagining.

The nonfiction writer with a story to tell always has another option at hand besides writing scenes with dialogue: you can describe the physical setting and summarize the narrative action briskly and forcefully. This was the preferred storytelling technique for centuries: see, for instance, the compressed tales of Stendhal or Kleist. So, when tempted to insert a scene in a nonfiction work that would require reconstructing it from imagination because you didn't observe it directly, my advice is, Don't do it unless you feel you absolutely have to. But if you are going to do it, you had better make damn sure that you do it artfully and discreetly—preferably by first telling us straight-out that you are in fact imagining it.

# Facts Have Implications: or,
# Is Nonfiction Really Fiction?

There is a notion going around these days that because
nonfiction is a construct, it is a fiction. To quote David
Shields's *Reality Hunger* (which is not necessarily to quote David
Shields, since he merrily appropriates authors' words for his
collaged text):

> "Fiction/nonfiction" is an utterly useless distinction. . . .
> There's a good case for arguing that any narrative account
> is a form of fiction. The moment you start to arrange the
> world in words, you alter its nature. The words themselves
> begin to suggest patterns and connections that seemed at
> the time to be absent from the events the words describe.
> Then the story takes hold. It begins to determine what
> goes in and what's left out. It has its own logic and it carries
> the writer along with it. He may well set out to write one
> story and find that he's writing quite another.

Now, the process described here certainly sounds like something every nonfiction writer has undergone, but I still am not

sure why the fact that one has selectively and self-consciously fashioned a text means that one has written fiction. An irony of Shields's stimulating if willfully perplexing book is that he professes to be bored by novels and short stories and to prefer reality, while at the same time insisting that nonfiction is really a fiction, of sorts.

He is not alone. There is a sense in which this has become the vanguard position. Recently, on a visit to Mexico, I had a conversation with two bright, young, philosophically trained Mexican essayists about the nature of the essay. They maintained that the personal essay, at least, should be classified as fiction—because the narrating self is a construction, because memory is unreliable and relies on imagination to fill in the gaps, and because many of the assertions in a personal essay cannot be tested or proven true. They both assumed I would be flattered by this reassignment, or at least agree that the principle was self-evident. But I held out for the idea that nonfiction, including personal essays, has a relationship to factual reality and self-testimony that makes it fundamentally different from fiction.

I fear that my hosts regarded me as intellectually naive, and rightly so: I get very soon out of my depth, philosophically speaking. But there must be a way for an amateur speculator like me, who is nevertheless a veteran essayist, to describe in words what my practice of nonfiction is and why I continue to believe so strenuously in that category as something separate from fiction (which I have also written, on occasion). "Reality" and "truth" are, of course, ambiguous notions, but still I find myself sitting at my computer, trying to home in closer and closer to the underlying shapes of experience. I have a conviction that life itself has forms underneath it: that there are connections to be made between experience and memory that are not purely subjective but that wait patiently to be brought to the surface. I intuit that life has a shape, has a meaning, and that by working to make a story come alive, a writer can happen upon these underlying configurations, arcs, or ovals. When memoirists or essayists follow closely on the trail of some developing suspense, and discover a through-line, meanwhile cutting away all irrelevancies, we are not fictionalizing, we are serving the innate shape of reality.

I realize this may sound like mystical mumbo jumbo: what I am calling "the innate shape of reality" may be nothing more than my aesthetic preferences, which always seek out the same tensions in raw experience, and then proceed to "discover" the same patterns underneath them. Still, I cling to the conviction that there is some organic thread to the things that happen to us, which lurks patiently in experience, hoping to be found out. It is a little like a potter throwing a pot and "feeling" the way the clay wants to go, or the architect Louis Kahn asking what the stones want to be, or Michelangelo carving into a piece of marble to find the shape waiting underneath. One doesn't have to be a genius like Michelangelo or Kahn to do this; all humble craftsmen know this moment when the form asserts itself.

The materials I am working with in nonfiction are facts and truths. I can record my thoughts and impressions, as long as I don't censor myself in advance; I can try to recapture memories as crisply as language will allow; and then I can ask myself whether what I have written comes down to the truth, feels true. If it doesn't I can keep going at it until I find the proper balance.

We often hear that what counts in good nonfiction is the literary, not the literal truth. In other words, it should not be necessary to stick to the actual facts, as long as we convey the underlying meaning, the artistic truth of the story one is trying to tell in a satisfying, powerful way. "What does it matter if Frey actually spent the few nights in prison he wrote about in his book?" asks Shields. "Fake jail time was merely a device to get a point across, a plausible situation in which to frame his suffering." I wonder. In my own experience, facts and truths are not so separate; they are often found walking hand in hand.

Facts are marvelous at delimiting and inscribing destinies. One is born and raised in New York City or Detroit or San Francisco, Odessa or Calcutta, and from that simple fact all sorts of consequences follow. One grows up in a Mormon or a Communist atheist household, raised by one or two parents, and so ensue more consequences. Facts have implications, which, it seems to me, are ignored at the nonfiction writer's peril. The whole plausibility of a nonfiction narrative may be undermined by altering or evading crucial details.

Let me give some examples. One of my students wanted to write about the failure of her marriage. But she did not want to tell readers right off—perhaps ever—that she discovered her husband was gay or bisexual. It was certainly her right to protect him, but the result was a muffled, baffling narrative.

Another student wanted to write about how prejudiced his fellow Austrians were: anti-Semitic, homophobic, racist, etc. He had known, and even been friendly with, various individuals who had had one or another of these prejudices but never all, and he thought it would be economical and more dramatic to combine them into a single composite bigot. The problem was that it seemed unlikely that the narrator-protagonist—who was coming across as intelligent, reasonable-voiced, humanistic—would ever befriend such a monster with so many disagreeable prejudices.

Someone else I knew was writing about her longtime platonic friendship with a gay man and combining him with another man who had been her ex-lover. If I had slept with someone, I could not imagine that fact not coloring or discoloring any future friendship—but that's me. Maybe there are people who can put it out of their minds. The point I'm making is not that she shouldn't write this nonfiction account with a composite character at the center, but that I could never do so. I realize many colleagues in the field, whose work I value highly, will disagree with me in this matter, and I have no problem with their bending the facts whenever it suits them. I am not a fundamentalist when it comes to deviating from factual circumstance, but whenever possible I myself *prefer* to tell the truth, which to my mind also means sticking to the facts. Making things up, bending the facts, throws off my attempt to get as close as possible to the shape underlying experience or to the psychology that flows from the precisely real.

When I am writing fiction, I am trying to get at the literary truth; when I am writing nonfiction, I aim for both the literary and literal truth. If that seems a restriction of my authorial freedom, it is a small price to pay for retaining belief in the wonderful, gruesome, uncanny shimmer of the facts as they play out in life.

# On the Ethics of
# Writing about Others

Whenever I speak in public about autobiographical nonfiction or simply give a reading of my own work, I am invariably asked in the Q & A session, "How should one deal with writing about one's family members or intimates? How does one balance the need to tell one's story with the pain others might feel in being exposed this way?" The assumption is that, since I have written candidly about family and friends in the past, I must know the answer to this difficult question. In fact I don't have a one-size-fits-all answer or a single set of rules. I continue to find the matter perplexing. I have to keep making up my mind on a case-by-case basis. And sometimes I get it wrong.

Let's first examine the common approaches to this dilemma. On the one hand, it is sometimes asserted that you have the right to tell your own story any way you want, and if you happen to offend some people by doing so, they're welcome to write their own stories. This strikes me as wishful thinking and a rationalization. We are *always* responsible for any pain our actions might give; and there is no "get out of jail" card from some professional writer or teacher that will relieve you of that burden. That does not mean you shouldn't go ahead and write the possibly offending material. It simply means that if you do, be prepared to accept the guilt, and don't try to weasel out of it by appealing to authorial license.

On the other hand, it is sometimes asserted, even by authorities as eminent as Joan Didion and Janet Malcolm, that writers are inherently betrayers, who will backstab everyone around them for a good line: if you go to bed with dogs, you wake up with fleas, and if you hang around writers enough, you will be traduced. This viewpoint strikes me also as an exaggeration. In fact, writers may be no more given to betrayal than those in other professions, such as politicians, undertakers, high school principals, florists . . . I have certainly decided many times to hold back from using juicy material if I thought it would damage the reputation of the person in question or deeply offend him or her.

Complicating the dilemma is that one does not always know what will cause offense. I have written fairly critically about people who seemed to have no problem with it. I have written somewhat negatively about people who ignored the main substance of my critique but pounced with outrage on some picayune detail they thought I got wrong. I have written glowingly about people who took it amiss, because they did not like the idea of having a walk-on cameo in my (center of the universe) story when they considered themselves as the center of the universe, or simply because they did not like the presumption that I could take their measure in a few paragraphs, regardless of how positively I ended up doing so. I have given offense to certain people by not writing about them when I wrote (critically) about their colleagues.

The issue at bottom is, Who am I to judge anyone? A fair-enough question. I'm someone who calls himself a writer, and if I write about my life, I am, inevitably, writing about others, because no man is an island. The main rules I give myself in doing so are: (1) Never write to settle scores. Enter into the other person's point of view, and be as fair-minded as possible; (2) Try to write as beautifully as possible, because well-wrought prose invites its own forgiveness—from you yourself, if not from the offended party.

When I first began writing about my family, I changed the names of my siblings but not my parents, reasoning, I suppose, that my parents were elderly and their lives were nearly over, whereas my siblings were still in the midst of the struggle. My father (the scapegoat of my family) was pleased that I had written about him at all, even though the portrait was by no means entirely flattering. My mother was touched that I'd written about her as a young woman, and said, "Now I know that you love me." (Typical of my mother that she would have ever doubted it.) When a second memoir essay of mine appeared several years later, however, she was shocked and said it was all untrue. I asked her what I'd gotten wrong. She paused and said they weren't lies exactly, but she was no longer like the young woman I'd portrayed, and why did I have to keep writing about that unhappy period (i.e., my childhood)? She forbade me ever to write about her again. I refused, saying that by this time she was a lively character whom I could render easily on the page, and I would make no guarantees. She said she would still come to my book party but would tell everyone I was her nephew, not her son.

Granted, writing about one's family or intimates can be an aggressive, vindictive act, but it can also be a way of communicating something to loved ones you never could before—a "gift" of the truth of your feelings. It can poison the air or clear it. In the end, my mother accepted what I had written about her, as did two of my siblings. But not the third, who still has not forgiven me after twenty years. And I didn't think I even treated her so shabbily on the page, nor did I use her real name. In retrospect,

I can see that particular sibling relationship was due to crash and burn, regardless.

Some writers get around the problem by showing their manuscript to the person being written about and asking if he or she objects to anything. I understand the scrupulosity of this position, but I could never do it myself. Having made the decision to go ahead and write about someone, and having done it to my satisfaction, I don't want to give that person such power! Once you invite people to make changes on your unpublished manuscript, they will. Besides, it's my moral dilemma, not theirs. Giving them the option to revise would be like shifting the ethical burden onto them.

Some creative writing professors advise their students that if the material seems too explosive, they should try writing it as fiction. I don't see this as a solution, since the person in question will most likely recognize the character based on him and still take offense. In short, the quandary remains obdurate; there are no easy answers.

Here, however, is one little trick that works for me. I like to tell myself that I am not a nice guy. In doing so, I prepare myself in advance for the anger that may be directed against me, and the guilt that I may have to endure for hurting someone else's feelings. (The funny thing is that by and large I *am* a nice guy, but I need the fiction that I'm not in order to sustain me in the act of writing.)

My final recommendations are:

1. Befriend only people who are too poor to hire lawyers to sue you.
2. If you plan to write about friendship, make lots of friends, because you are bound to lose a few.
3. For the same reason, try to come from a large family.

# Modesty and Assertion

## 1. Developing One's Voice

The most difficult hurdle confronting the would-be essayist or memoirist is the fear that one's own life story, one's experiences, ideas, and impressions are of too little importance to pass on. "Why should I talk about my happy or unhappy childhood? Or my appreciation of nature? Why burden other people with the unsettled debris of my mind?" thinks the student.

These doubts must be successfully overcome if you are to write, but how? Certainly it is important to study literary forms and techniques, as a way to liberate the indecisive imagination. Yet no amount of craft can substitute for the sense that you have something to say worth heeding. Without it, the results can be that safe, evasive writing workshop piece composed of fragments that allude to personal pain but leave out the nitty-gritty details, or that plays hide-and-seek through an excessively clotted surface.

To be a writer is a monstrously arrogant act. It presumes that you should be listened to for pages on end. But at the same time that elementary and secondary schools are pressured to turn out better writers (or at least better SAT essay test takers), there is much in the culture that stands ready to clip the wings of arrogance, mute assertion, and encourage speedy consensus. Consider the high school environment: teenagers are constantly checking each other to make sure they are not too out of line to fit in. Nothing is worse than to be deemed an oddball, crazy, strange. Added to this peer coercion is the pressure from teachers to study hard but not let your accomplishments go to your head.

I know that when I was in high school I seemed to be in a continual battle with adults to justify my budding self-esteem against charges that I was getting swell-headed. When I was admitted to a good college, I was told, "You're a big fish in a little pond here, but no one will notice you there. Every one of those kids is a brain and most of them are a lot smarter than you." Clearly I must have been something less than an angel to have provoked such vindictive prognoses. My high school teachers would have been happy to learn that in my first year or so at college I *was* invisible, and it made me miserable. They might have also been surprised to learn how much I doubted my talents. I didn't think I was smart enough to be a writer. True, I would have liked more than anything to join the literary ranks, but to me they were gods, they wrote superhuman books like *The Brothers Karamazov* and *Anna Karenina*. Their brains were filled with original concepts, they had sampled all of life; in short, what was going on in their heads was not going on in mine. So I entered college a prelaw major, thinking I would *assist* writers by specializing in copyright law.

As it happened, I had very little to say to the other prelaw students in my freshman class, whereas when I hung out with the would-be writers, conversation flowed. Moreover, these would-be writers did not seem significantly smarter than I was. I had still not received a sign from above to choose the literary path, no bush had burst into flames as I strode College Walk, and I sincerely doubted that I had one of those fertile, all-inclusive minds to become one of the elect, but in the meantime, just for fun, I wrote a few stories and showed them around. By my senior year I was editing the college literary magazine. I felt as though I were feigning a part, but what I would come to learn was that bluffing is an integral part of becoming a writer: you bluff and you bluff, until one day the world starts to treat you like a writer, and you think (you are the last one to think it), "Well, maybe I actually am one," still feeling mentally puny. But by now you are more adept at hiding such shameful thoughts.

This notion that a writer needs superhuman intelligence may sound far-fetched, but I encountered a similar attitude in others. When I got married for the first time, at twenty, my father-in-law, a Viennese émigré psychoanalyst who understandably had doubts about my ability to take care of his daughter when I told him of my intention to become a writer, took me aside after the wedding celebration and said, "In every century there are maybe three minds capable of literary genius. In the nineteenth century it was Goethe, Balzac, and Tolstoy. In the twentieth century, Proust, Joyce . . . maybe Rilke or Mann. If you find writing too difficult, you can always make a living at television or something like that." Then he put his arm around me and said, "I have complete faith in you," meaning, I have confidence that you will give up this foolishness when you realize that you are not one of the three.

All these dire ill-wishers, telling me I couldn't make it, were constantly popping up in my path when I was young: they only reinforced my stubbornness. I remember one summer, working as a guard at the Metropolitan Museum, talking to another museum guard who studied Zen. He asked me what my goal in life was. I said, "I want to become a great writer." He answered, "Then you will never become a great writer, because if you strive for greatness you will not attain it." Thanks a lot, man! Of course he was right in the sense that I became not a great writer but a decent one. And someday I may write something great. Why deny myself the possibility? You must cherish in your heart the possibility that you *could* become the writer of your age: world-historical ambitions are needed to keep scribbling and turning out manuscript copy.

Have you ever seen two writers of medium reputation being introduced to each other for the first time? Each is probably thinking, "How can he be a writer? I am the writer." Each sees himself as the emperor of an unrecognized kingdom. It is like that case of the three mental patients in Ypsilanti State Hospital, each with the unshakable conviction that he was Jesus Christ, even after being put together with the other two who had the same delusion.*

Over the years I have learned something that contradicts my prior elevated assumptions about the literary profession. I have met dozens of writers, and some of them are not very bright. But they get by somehow: they have a knack, survivor's instincts, the canny ability to foreground what they do best, an in with the zeitgeist. It turns out you don't have to be that smart to be a writer.

What you do need, however, is a tone of assertion.

I sometimes think you can make the reader accept almost anything if you back it up with strong-enough conviction. Take these lines by Pablo Neruda, from his poem "There Is No Forgetfulness":

> If you ask me where I have been
> I have to say, "It so happens . . ."
> I have to talk about the earth turned dark with stones,
> and the river which ruins itself by keeping alive;
> I only know about objects that birds lose,
> the sea far behind us, or my sister crying.

---

*_The Three Christs of Ypsilanti_, by Milton Rokeach, 1964, reprinted by New York Review Classics.

Or this passage from Neruda's poem "Nothing But Death":

I'm not sure, I understand only a little, I can hardly see,
but it seems to me that its singing has the color of damp
   violets,
because the face of death is green,
and the look death gives is green. . . .
Death is inside the folding cots:
it spends its life sleeping on the slow mattresses

Neruda is always saying, in effect, I don't know this but I do know that, and I have seen with my own eyes $x$ and $y$ and $z$. So what if many of the facts he purports to swear by are fantastic? He has learned to season his surreal images with the plausible verbal formulae of someone bearing witness; it is these rhetorical assertions of the limits of his knowledge that make his metaphoric visions easier to accept. Neruda comes straight out of Whitman, who boldly asserted, "I was the man . . . I suffered . . . I was there."

The oldest poetic tradition in the world is the chant of assertion, which one finds in almost every tribal lore: "This is what happened" or "This [i.e., rain] is what we want to have happen" or "Our god can make such-and-such miracles happen." No academic hedging, no "perhaps" or "under certain circumstances" or "It would seem to be the case that . . ." Good writers down through the ages have known how to cut through the thickness of complexity when it suited them and simply declare. The turn toward aphorism frequently signals this intention.

Sometimes a writer may even bring into existence, through assertion, more wisdom than he or she possessed before beginning to write the sentence. To put it another way: the words themselves, by having been placed in their most compact formulation, generate, side by side, magnetic reactions amongst themselves that release unforeseen meanings. Good writers are always trying to write *above* their heads, to hit on understandings beyond their conscious knowledge, through fortuitous word choice. F. Scott Fitzgerald, a writer of clearly superior intelligence, was superb at precociously rolling out an inflection of weary wisdom: his elegiac stance of looking back at life from the other shore, "the far side of paradise," and his comfortable command of generalization and the generational first-person plural, produced a prose that sounded unfailingly wise—whereas there is some doubt, after reading biographies of his life, that he actually possessed such scores of sagacity.

I do not want to imply that narrative conviction is nothing more than a technique. However, I do think that what the professional knows is that there are days when the mental cupboard is rather bare, but you can still get by with a tone of assertion.

I had some experience with this sort of bluffing in my twenties, when I supported myself for several years as a ghostwriter. Most of my work was done for people in the social sciences: hospital administrators who still needed to project a scholarly presence, psychologists solicited for book reviews in academic journals, chairmen of educational departments who were called upon to give speeches. I knew next to nothing about these fields, and so in the beginning I would try to elicit from my employers their own ideas on the subject, only to discover that they had none; that was why they were hiring a ghostwriter. After a few days of library research, I knew a little more about different sides of the issue in question and could bluff the rest. I found that even more than concocting fresh ideas (which were beyond my grasp in any case, since I lacked sufficient expertise) was perfecting the tone of a courtly, skeptical, worldly professional who has seen the intellectual fashions come and go. How hard I worked to capture the ponderous wit of middle-aged social scientists! Once,

I stayed up half the night honing a ploddingly facetious jest with which to begin a paper to be delivered at the American Psychological Association by a man of color thirty-five years older than myself. And how I enjoyed inserting the line that began "As an African-American, I feel confident in saying that . . ." Ghostwriting is a much-maligned profession. Not only can you pad the hours; not only is it good practice for fiction writing, enabling you to inhabit other characters; but it is also excellent training for nonfiction, teaching the importance, the timbre, the pitch of assertion at all costs.

The first time I was assigned to write a review for *The New York Times Book Review*, I found myself again in the situation of having to invent a persona: to pretend to be this cultivated, self-assured, supremely balanced arbiter who had only a glancing relationship to my everyday self. I reached back to my ghostwriting training—as indeed I have often done when commissioned to write a piece for this or that periodical, each time taking into account the publication's specific readership and adjusting my writer's voice accordingly. If this makes me sound like a chameleon or a charlatan, it is no more than any of us do when recalibrating our presentation of self for a local barbecue, a fancy cocktail party, a parent-teacher conference, or a salary review meeting with the boss. Meanwhile, the more I took to writing personal essays, the more experienced I became in projecting in print the appearance of a stable, unitary self—a core around which the different elected tonalities of the moment could spin.

Let me try to tie together a few strands. I began with the problem that I did not have enough confidence in what I had to say. Then I discovered that there could never be a single "I" who could speak for me, I could only communicate an aspect of myself: sometimes more friendly, sometimes more contrarian. Whichever path I chose could never reveal my entire self: the linearity of language made that impossible. Yet this limitation proved liberating, because no matter what I said, it wouldn't be "me," exactly, but at best an approximation, like a ghostwriter channeling another's voice, I felt freer to speak.

At the same time, I discovered the importance of sincerity and conviction, of that tone of assertion necessary to put across what I had to say. It was not trickery: I wanted to be sincere and direct. But gradually I understood that I could only do so within the context of a partial projection of my whole self: a sincerity within an insincerity. In exploring these fragmented sides of myself, I also found that I had something to talk about. I found that I had a "voice," and a story.

I put the word *voice* timidly in quotes, because, as you will see from this satiric, cautionary poem by Ron Padgett, the whole concept can be problematic:

## Voice

I have always laughed
when someone spoke of a young writer
"finding his voice." I took it
literally: had he lost his voice?
Had he thrown it and had it
not returned? Or perhaps they
were referring to his newspaper
*The Village Voice?* He's trying
to find his *Voice*.
　　What isn't
funny is that so many young writers
seem to have found this notion
credible: they set off in search
of their voice, as if it were

a single thing, a treasure
difficult to find but worth
the effort. I never thought
such a thing existed. Until
recently. Now I know it does.
I hope I never find mine. I
wish to remain a phony the rest of my life.

## 2. Storytelling

A storytelling impulse runs similarly through my personal essays and other nonfiction. The starting point is usually trying to render justice to an actual experience. I have a desire (see "Facts Have Implications") to find the shape underlying ordinary happenings, through pressing them into artful form. It is almost as if by relating an experience in a coherent, suspenseful, attention-getting way, I have mastered its meaning. Of course I probably haven't, but I'm no longer so confused and disturbed by it.

The storytelling penchant may be a natural gift: I'd like to give my work ethic credit for it, but I suspect it was always in me. We all know people, often very bright, who can't seem to tell an anecdote intelligibly—they start off in one place, backtrack, apologize, keep losing the point, then fumble the dramatic punch line—while others seem to be born raconteurs who can gather a crowd around them at parties and improvise the merest nothing into an amusing narrative. Part of the storytelling ability is simply the anticipation of boredom and the introduction of a sudden heightening or surprise. To be a good storyteller you need to have first internalized the audience: that subvocal groan that says, "Okay, okay, get on with it." Not that you always have to cater to the audience's expectations: you can cross them up, frustrate them, prolong their tension, though that too can be a way of entertaining them. In any case, you have to be aware of their demands, whether you satisfy them or not.

Walter Benjamin, in his 1936 essay "The Storyteller," argued that the art of storytelling was coming to an end: "Less and less frequently do we encounter people with the ability to tell a tale properly. More and more often there is embarrassment all around when the wish to hear a story is expressed. It is as if something that seemed inalienable to us, the securest among our possessions, were taken from us: the ability to exchange experiences. . . . Was it not noticeable at the end of the war that men returned from the battleground silent—not richer, but poorer in communicable experience?" Benjamin attributed this atrophy in part to the decline of the artisan class: those master craftsmen, traveling journeymen, seamen, and so on who went out into the world, where they gathered experience and then told stories to their apprentices while working together at a slow, repetitious task. An interesting speculation: who knows if it's true? We can at least agree with Benjamin when he says that modern life, with its assembly lines, shocks, fragmented work processes, and information overload, makes it harder to re-create the sort of leisurely talking and listening environment that passing on stories requires.

Benjamin sums up the storyteller as follows: "Seen in this way, the storyteller joins the ranks of the teachers and sages. He has counsel—not for a few situations, as the proverb does, but for many, like the sage. For it is granted to him to reach back to a whole lifetime (a life, incidentally, that comprises not only his own experience but no little of the experience of others; what the storyteller knows from hearsay is added to his own). His gift is the ability to relate his life; his distinction, to be able to tell his entire life. The storyteller: he is the man who could let the wick of his life be consumed completely by the gentle flame of his story. . . . The novel is significant, therefore, not because it presents someone else's fate to us, perhaps didactically, but because this stranger's fate by virtue of the flame which consumes it yields us the warmth which we never draw from our own fate. What draws the reader to the novel is the hope of warming his shivering life with a death he reads about."

For Benjamin, it would seem, the storyteller descends from the old Homeric oral performer in the tribal circle or marketplace, down to the teller of succinct, uncanny tales (he specifically mentions Poe, Leskov, and Stevenson), and finally to the novelist who furnishes the spark of mortality. What, then, of the personal essayist, the memoirist, the creative nonfiction writer? If I, for instance, call myself a storyteller, it is not because I consider myself a sage, but because I make it a point to try to tell my entire life—albeit in a way in which Benjamin would have disapproved. He insisted that good storytelling should suppress explanation and psychological analysis. Show, don't tell. Whereas I love to put in explanation and analysis, even when it verges on rationalization: it so happens that rationalization is what two-thirds of my stories are about.

It is sometimes recommended that you should wait a period of years—some say fifteen, some say five—before you write about an actual experience, but I'm too impatient. As I go about my daily life, I'm turning it into a story. If something peculiar happens to me at the grocery store or the dry cleaners, I already start shaping it into a narrative the moment I'm out the door, and I bring it home to my wife the way a cat presents a captured mouse to its master. If my wife has news of her own she wants to tell first, I am very put out, though I try to hide it, because here is this gift of an anecdote nicely shaped, dripping from my mouth.

A psychotherapist might find drawbacks to this method: by turning my life so quickly into a story, I fail to live in the moment, fail to enjoy life to the fullest, and I set up a barrier of detachment between myself and others. I must admit that I have never felt any discomfit in being a detached person (I've never been any other way, so I don't miss it), but I've probably discomfited others, loved ones especially, who might have wanted me more engaged. Another danger in this method is that by making life immediately into a story, I might be mythologizing—lying to myself, for the sake of reassurance and ego flattery—to such an extent that the lies harden and become permanent. It is sometimes said that psychotherapy helps a patient make a "tellable myth" out of his or her past life, though I assume what is meant by that is a narrative not only capable of being related but shorn of self-deception. When I write about an experience, what I try to do is to correct the sins of the ego by analyzing what happened, dissecting my own motives, and putting myself in the other person's shoes. I can't say I actually correct my distortions by self-analysis—the very term "self-analysis" sounds like an invitation to the mining of fool's gold—but I make what I hope is a good-faith attempt.

Often, what will start me on the hunt for a story (or an explanation—they practically come to the same thing in my mind) is an unresolved moment, a mysterious gesture or comment that nags at me. Why did F. say that cutting remark at the party? Why was I so insensitive and rude to G.? To give an example: I was having lunch several years ago with a learned colleague of mine, an elderly professor of whom I was very fond. As we left the building where he has an office next to mine, he had thought of going back for his umbrella, but I assured him that if it started to rain while we were at lunch, I would share my umbrella with him. Sure enough, it started to rain while we were sitting in the restaurant. As we headed back to campus, rounding out what had been a highly enjoyable conversation, I kept trying to ensure that he would be fully covered by my umbrella, and he kept drifting out of its reach; the left shoulder of his blue tweed sports jacket was catching all sorts of raindrops. As we entered the campus gates, he pointed to the door of our building, which was about fifty yards away, and said, "I can take it from here, you don't have to walk with me anymore." I said, "Of course I'll walk you," since I was going in that direction anyway and since I wanted to prolong our time together as much as possible, but I noticed that he was determined to leave me at the campus gates and go on alone the last fifty yards. He patted my arm good-naturedly and set off.

Now why did he do that? I began wondering. Had I said something during lunch that offended him? Search my memory as I might, nothing came to mind—and besides, I don't think this particular man would have chosen that way to express his displeasure. Did he, being older, chafe at the suggestion that he needed my protection, and did he want to demonstrate his complete self-reliance and lack of frailty? Or did he simply like walking in the rain; did it have romantic associations for him? Or was he rebuking me for the clumsy way I had handled my assignment of holding the umbrella over him thus far? Or did he want to return to an envelope of solitude, however much he might have enjoyed my company? That I could certainly understand. Maybe he didn't know how to put the request for privacy into tactful words at that moment.

I found myself thinking about different styles of terminating an interaction. I tend to be abrupt myself, even wounding others by failing to provide a cozy, fuzzy, prolonged good-bye—refusing, that is, to pretend that I could not bear to leave the other person, when often I was more than reconciled to embarking on my next activity. But my colleague was more of a gentleman than I; he was from the South, had better manners. Could his gesture of patting my arm have had something to do with his upbringing? Something regional? Or generational? It reminded me of the reserved and somewhat withdrawn quality I had seen in other southern and southwestern writers of a certain age. What *was* that? . . . The long and short of it was, I never did figure out what to make of his stand. But I jotted it down in my diary, to puzzle over later, maybe to use in an essay or give to a character in a short story.

He died some years back. Now all I have of him is this memory of our parting at the campus gates, and his going on alone. Is it a story?

# On Writers' Journals

The tenth-century Japanese court lady Sei Shonagon kept a writer's notebook in which she recorded a miscellaneous catchall of things charming and annoying, rhapsodic descriptions of nature, odd facts, and malicious observations of her countrymen. She claimed to be chagrined when it was discovered and read, though a part of her must at least subconsciously have had readers in mind all along. Now considered an indispensable classic, Shonagon's *Pillow Book* was also, in a sense, the ancestor of the modern blog.

Writing is one way of self-making. That a would-be author often nurtures to life a professional literary voice, as Sei Shonagon did, through the act of keeping a notebook, is a phenomenon to which many writers have borne witness. The writer's notebook has been variously compared to a laboratory, a mirror, a brainstorming tool, an icebreaker, a wailing wall, a junk drawer, a confessional, a postcard to oneself, a singing in the shower, a jump-start cable, an aide-mémoire, an archive, an anthology, a warehouse, a tourist's camera, a snooping device, a sharpener of observation, a survival kit, a way of documenting mental illness, a meditation practice, a masturbation, a therapist, a spiritual adviser, a compost bin, a punching bag, a sounding board, a friend.

Writers characteristically express gratitude to their journals, as though the fact of these volumes' coming to be filled with words were an accident of grace performed by some genie while they slept. Occasionally they may utter resentment or fear of surrendering one's life to journal keeping, of being lured into hypergraphic addiction. And uncertainties linger over the practice: should the notebook be spiral or bound, handwritten or a computer file? Done every day or only when the mood strikes? Performed privately at home or in a library or café? Is a writer's journal a separate literary genre, to be parsed by scholars, or only a more pretentious term for a diary?

Freedom is the giddy promise of writers' journals: freedom to try out things, to write clumsy sentences when no one is looking, to be prejudiced, even stupid. No one can expect to write well who will not first take the risk of writing badly. The writer's notebook is a safe place for such experiments.

I have been keeping a writer's journal ever since I was seventeen. It fills more than thirty notebooks of all sizes and covers, and every time I've moved I have had to lug around that pile, then find a place to store them in file cabinets and closets. I never put them on open bookshelves, because I wouldn't want a visitor opening one at random and reading, perhaps, about himself.

I have tried out a variety of syntactical and tonal maneuvers in these pages—the writer's journal can strengthen technique the way that finger exercises do a pianist's—but overall, I have opted for the least self-conscious formulation. The diaries are my first line of written storytelling. I note down things that happen very quickly, without trying for art: often it's late, my hand is tired, I'm just trying to record an experience or thought as directly as possible. The majority of these diary items turn out to be useless fragments, narrative torsos, incomplete meditations or failed stories, but I'm never sure when I pick up my pen to write in my diary whether whatever I'm trying to set down is going to have a satisfying narrative shape or not. Sometimes I find the shape in the middle of describing: I get the point suddenly. At other times it takes years of unconscious sifting.

I went through a phase (happily short) when my hastily scribbled journal prose seemed to me more honest, fresh, and representative of my inner nature than my intentionally wrought prose. I conceived a project of plowing through my journals and excerpting the best parts to make a fat book. But I did not get very far: I bogged down around the period of my early twenties, when I couldn't stand to listen anymore to the callow fellow I was then; and when I jumped ahead chronologically, I was again put off, feeling a combination of boredom and chagrin. It seemed these journals were not as densely packed with goodies as I had imagined.

Occasionally I go back, painful as it is, to peek at my first "writer's notebook": at seventeen I was hardly a writer but trying on the persona to see if it would fit. At the time I was reading Nietzsche and Dostoevsky and thinking dark adolescent thoughts. I may also have been influenced by Gide's *Journals*, since he was another of my early models. In any case, I note how quickly I was drawn to the aphoristic form, which allowed me to see if I had any worthy thoughts by daring me to express them as concisely and analytically as possible. Here are a few typically pretentious entries:

> *The unreal feeling that strangers are doing things for my entertainment. People pass me and break into laughter at a dramatically opportune moment.*

*Perhaps I view all people as objects, not real human beings. The writer knows people less than others. He builds up an image of a person by painstakingly gathering psychological and external data. (Is this statement true? Is it only that the writer doesn't know people well, but he knows them more than anyone else?) My friend M.'s distinction between knowing a person and knowing about a person (the latter is tied to existing vicariously rather than living one's own life). M. says: Knowing another person is feeling another person. (But how? Be more specific.)*

Odd how early one's themes are set in place. Particularly in the last entry, I see the naming of a fault, followed by rationalization and self-aggrandizement (it's because I'm a writer), followed by the bald assertion of a paradox that challenges conventional wisdom (the writer knows people less than others), followed by self-doubt, the citing of a friend's contrary opinion, followed by unease about my capacity to feel. Eventually, these abstract probings into my psyche and its discontents gave way to more anecdotal entries. There were also brainstorms for novel or film plots which, fortunately, never got further than being jotted down. But however dopey or vulgar the plot was, I still had to enter it in my journal, if for no other reason than to get rid of it. I had decided from the start that in my journals I would not censor myself or try to appear more enlightened or mature than I felt. As a consequence, I have often come across as more immature in my journal pages than anywhere else. There I would complain, settle scores, be unfair, have the last say. The journals are not a wholly accurate portrait of myself, overemphasizing as they do my antisocial voice, muttering what I would not dare say aloud.

In my first journal-keeping years, I would often vent feelings. But one day, reading over the journals in sequence, I discovered that I was massively repeating myself, because I didn't have more than a half-dozen emotions. So I began "expressing myself" less and documenting the world more: I would write down long discussions after they took place, or note the quirks in a friend's speech patterns, or describe the décor of an acquaintance's apartment. This period corresponded with a phase of writing poetry, during which I was trying hard to pay attention, live in the moment. I was schooling myself in the concrete. For instance, I would enter a notation that a woman I was dating always kept cherry sodas in her refrigerator, partly in the hope that, years from then, when I came to write about her, this detail would jog my memory and bring back other specifics.

By this time, I knew I was a writer, so I started self-consciously retooling the journal for later use. I was like a squirrel hiding away nuts for an older me who would raid the stash. The fact that I often forgot what I had written in the journals made my finding a tasty morsel all the more pleasing years after.

In 1968, I went to work for Teachers & Writers Collaborative as a poet in the schools, teaching children and teenagers creative writing. One of the job's requirements was to keep a journal of classroom experiences. Many writers in the program tended to dodge that task by turning in perfunctory, minimal entries, but the poet Ron Padgett and I saw it as a golden opportunity to sort out the jumbled excitement of trying to teach a class full of kids. We competed for who could write the longest diary entries. At this point I was thus keeping two sets of journals, one for Teachers & Writers and one, focused more on my private life, for myself. Sometimes I felt ridiculous spending half my life writing down what I had done, instead of going out and living more. Still, I remain grateful for the discipline of keeping teaching diaries, which formed the basis of my first book of prose, *Being with Children*.

My next book of prose was a novel, *Confessions of Summer*, which was largely autobiographical, more or less based on the woman who kept cherry sodas in her refrigerator. I went back over my writer's journals from the period when I was dating her and pulled out certain nuggets, which I put together into a chapter called "Journal of Decrystallization" (alluding to Stendhal's theories on love and its crystallization).

I still thought of myself as half a poet, half a novelist, when my literary career took a strange turn in the late 1970s: I fell in love with the personal essay. Since then I have been increasingly identified with this form—and indeed, I think of myself as a personal essayist above all else. I have also found there to be an intimate, direct connection between journal writing and personal essays, more so than with any work I'd previously done in other genres. A paragraph entry might contain an insight that could serve as the springboard for a later essay. In a pinch, with a deadline looming, I could even cobble together a personal essay out of several journal entries on the same subject. Both types of writing are nonfiction, often autobiographical, relaxed, conversational, relying on unfolding thought processes. The difference is that you can get away with the fragment in a journal, while a personal essay has to add up to something more.

The truth is that the more confident I have become at personal essay writing, the less I have kept writer's journals. In recent years I tend to bypass the note-taking stage and go directly to essay writing, utilizing the very uncertainty I may have about a topic at the onset as part of my subject matter. But I still sporadically keep writer's journals, and I still raid my old journals in the service of whatever individual writing I happen to be attempting. So, when I embarked on a long, difficult personal essay about my father, shortly before his death, I took it as far as I could go on my own, then started leafing through the journals, looking for any entries in which he had made an appearance. I ended up using, with only slight changes, a few items as reliable witnesses, mostly from the later period when he was in a nursing home, and these were transferred bodily from the private journal to the finished essay.

I still have a fantasy of getting a grant someday to keep a daily journal for a year and publishing the results as a book. (How honest would I permit myself to be?) I also fantasize getting a grant and hiring some impecunious graduate student to computerize all my writer's notebooks, indexing them and making them accessible to hyperlinks, so that I can pursue various strands of memory at leisure in my retirement. Perhaps by that point I will have become doddering enough to overcome my earlier nausea at examining in detail the person I was. Gertrude Stein says somewhere that those traits of ours which most embarrass us when we are young, we later come to see as our charms.

Above all, the writer's notebook invokes the muse, invites thought. Here we might note the phonic similarity between *muse* and *musing*. The mother of the Muses is Mnemosyne, goddess of memory; by writing down what you would otherwise forget, even willingly forget, you summon your better self (the muse)— or your worse—with these intimate scribbles.

# The Essay:
## Exploration or Argument?

For years I have been saying that the essay is not a logical proof or a legal brief, it does not have to persuade, what is important is to follow one's thoughts, even if they lead to contradiction. In my introduction to *The Art of the Personal Essay* I quoted Professor William Zeiger, who cited Montaigne as the essayist's exemplary model: "He did not argue or try to persuade. He had no investment in winning over his audience to his opinion; accordingly, he had no fear of being refuted. On the contrary, he expected that some of the ideas he expressed would change, as they did in later essays." The essay, I insisted, was an open-ended adventure, an invitation to doubt and self-surprise: it was precisely those unexpected turns that would lift the prose and make it sing. Conversely, if you know already what all your points are going to be when you sit down to write, the piece is likely to seem dry, dead on arrival.

I still don't disagree with the above statements, but over the years I have been rethinking my basic position. For one thing, I've noticed that when my students write essays that simply follow their thoughts without any spine of argument, the texts don't cohere, don't satisfy. For another, I've come to realize that my own essays do always contain an implicit argument and make an attempt to persuade (or at least seduce, entertain, distract the reader into amusement, which are other means of persuasion, ones that Montaigne was himself happy to use). Even when I set out with no end in sight, I still am aware as I am writing when an argument is building underneath, and I nudge the prose along in ways that will accentuate that architecture.

I feel hypocritical urging my students not to worry too much about the argumentative, logical, structural props even as I use these same props to steer my own "open-ended" explorations. In pedagogic self-defense, I would say that it is more important, in the early stages, for student essayists to court uncensored thoughts and potentially enriching digressions—to generate masses of pages, in short—than to be uptight about organizing a thesis statement, three paragraphs of argument, and a conclusion. In fact, it puts unreasonable pressure on students to ask them to generate a thesis before they have explored their thoughts on the page. On a more confessional level, I admit that one reason I find it hard to teach the intuitive rhetorical techniques that govern my own essays is that I don't always know how to name or describe them, except in fumbling, mumbling ways.

Here we come to one of the dirty secrets, or let us say one of the challenges, in teaching creative nonfiction: the creative writing teacher, whose authority extends from being a practitioner of the form, is usually not a trained rhetorician. Unlike the poet-teacher, who can draw on a traditional lexicon of metrical and formal terms, the nonfiction writer-teacher is left to grab at such ad-hoc distinctions as are currently being worked out piecemeal, belatedly, and absent a unifying theory: for example, Vivian Gornick's *The Situation and the Story*, Carl Klaus's *The Made-Up Self*,

David Shields' *Reality Hunger*, John D'Agata's *The Lost Origins of the Essay*, Patricia Hampl's *I Could Tell You Stories*, or my own humble efforts. We are in almost complete ignorance of the centuries of rhetorical terminology that extend all the way back to classical Greece and Rome.

Let us go back to that moment in the 1970s and 1980s when the split occurred between composition and the personal essay, and try to understand it better. Coming out of the 1960s, with its emphasis on "relevance," were programs such as the Voice Project at Stanford University, led by John Hawkes and Albert J. Guérard, which sought to renovate the teaching of freshman composition by emphasizing autobiographical writing (getting students to find their own "voice"). I was sympathetic to such efforts, because in my own college education I had been turned off to the essay: it had been taught in freshman composition mainly as a way to hone argumentative skills and defend a position in an academic paper or debate. It took me years to discover the glories of the essay, by reading Hazlitt, Lamb, Montaigne, Baldwin, Orwell, Woolf, etc., and coming to see it as a perfect vehicle for the display of belletristic sensibility and unique personality. As a result, when I began teaching the essay myself, I seized on this concept that it was not a legal brief, nor an argument, but an exploration. I wanted to rescue the essay from freshman comp and restore it to its rightful place in the literary canon.

There may have been another, less attractive reason, for such a rescue effort: the status differential between composition and creative writing. The freshman comp instructor is the dray horse of the university, often working for adjunct wages, forced to teach many sections, obliged to deal with students from other majors who have no interest in the subject, and required to follow a rigidly predetermined curriculum. Indeed, many MFA writing students begin their teaching careers as composition instructors, dreaming of the day when they can publish enough to be assigned creative writing workshops.

Tenured professors of creative writing are for the most part not obliged to teach composition. We teach in a looser, less methodical fashion, and we are more inclined to mystify our subject, to make like a magus holding the secrets of literary art. In my case that impressionistic delivery is partly a way to disguise my ignorance: I am ashamed of not knowing Latin or the precise rhetorical terms underpinning my intuitive prose practice. I envy writers of the previous generation, such as Mary McCarthy, for whom Latin was a requirement in secondary school, and whose flexible conversational style is inflected by a starch that gives their sentences *gravitas* and sinuosity. Not to mention propulsive argumentation. I also envy professors of rhetoric their knowledge. As the classicist Victoria Kahn has maintained, "we do desperately need new ways of recovering the insights of classical and early modern writers about eloquent speech."

I once shared my introduction to *The Art of the Personal Essay* with a learned English department colleague who pronounced it "charming," which I took to mean insufficiently theorized and dilettantish. From time to time I tell myself I must take a course in Latin, or at least thoroughly familiarize myself with Quintilian's and Cicero's books of rhetoric in translation and meanwhile catch up on some modern rhetorical theory. But I don't; I'm too lazy. Instead I continue to pursue an untutored love of syntax. When I see sentences such as *Just as X and Y, so Z;* or *Not A, not B, not C, but D*, I try to imitate them, just for the fun of it. Imitation used to be a respected pedagogic technique but has fallen undeservedly into disuse, replaced by an unrealistic emphasis on "originality." In fact, by trying to imitate a writer you admire and falling short of the mark, you may discover, in the gap between your efforts and hers, traces of your own original style.

In any case, copious reading for pleasure and the occasional self-conscious imitation can do wonders in stretching one's syntactical variety. (Those who would like a more systematic approach, from alliteration to zeugma, might consult *Figures of Speech* by Arthur Quinn, or *Writing with Clarity and Style: A Guide to Rhetorical Devices for Contemporary Writers* by Robert A. Harris.

I also find it a good idea to plant knots of tension in the body of the essay and try to untie them along the way, by way of constructing a skeletal argument. The pressure to answer such internalized-reader questions as "Why are you telling us all this?" and "What are you getting at?" can help drive an essay, can give it pleasurable suspense and forward momentum.

Plato attacked the teachers of rhetoric for wanting to win an argument more than uncover moral truth and compared their skill to that of pastry cooks. Maybe his distaste for casuistry is where our modern mistrust of rhetorical devices originated. Still, who was more adept at maintaining an argument than Plato? It used to puzzle me that Georg Lukács, in his meaty "On the Nature and Form of the Essay," cited Plato's *Dialogues* next to Montaigne as "the writings of the greatest essayists." How could a dialogue be an essay? I wondered, literal-mindedly. But I am coming to think that all good essays are dialogues, and all partake of both exploration and argumentation.

# The Made-Up Self:
# On the Difficulty of Turning
# Oneself into a Character

The idea that personal essayists and memoirists construct a persona would seem to be self-evident. In *The Made-Up Self*, Carl H. Klaus has given us an excellent, nuanced, and very useful elaboration of that historical process. I said much the same in my previous essay, "On the Necessity of Turning Oneself into a Character," and so I was delighted when I read Klaus's book. And yet, asked to speak about this self-evident phenomenon today, I find myself hesitating and entertaining objections. Why is that? Am I such a contrarian that I must argue with my own understanding and the collective wisdom of my fellow panelists? There is that, but I think it goes further. I do not remember ever having concocted this made-up self; I can't recall the night when, like Geppetto fabricating his Pinocchio, I stayed up late and finished off the puppet that would stand in for me.

On the contrary: what impresses and appalls me is how little I seem to be able to change my everyday personality, not to mention my writing style. I have been writing with literary intent for half a century, and for the most part, my I-persona has remained fairly constant. Even the papers I wrote in college show many traces of characteristic syntactical constructions, tones of voice, argumentation, and strategies that have followed me around and still infect my writing. When you add to that the fact that I continue to make the same interpersonal mistakes in my domestic life, in my friendships, in my handling of students, despite the embarrassment they have caused me and the pain they have caused others, I have to wonder how much is in my control and how much is not.

The United States has often been characterized as a generator of self-invention. How could it be otherwise, when so many immigrants cut their ties with the social stratification of the Old Country and began what they hoped was a new, more fluid life, aiming to fulfill their dreams on these shores? Nineteenth-century America saw a plague of con artists who passed themselves off as counts and dukes, in the absence of a national aristocracy: they were merely the gaudiest representatives of that tendency toward self-invention that enveloped large swatches of the population. So yes, we as a people are receptive to the idea of a made-up self. Contrast that with Europe, where the very idea that one has a self, made up or otherwise, is contested. Continental cultural criticism seems more inclined to view the self as a social construct, an aggregate of mass media inputs and political indoctrinations. In this regard I instinctively side with the American viewpoint: yes, I am an individual and I damned well have a self, which I rely on with comfort and consolation—though I just can't recall how I came by it.

Many people like to think that they are radically different from their parents, that they took a separate path of self-invention, so to speak, sometime around adolescence. I consider this posture arrogant and ungrateful. Like it or not, I see both my parents when I look in the mirror, and their genes, their habits, even their lousy posture have taken up room in me. Certainly, I am not the same as my parents or my siblings, but even taking into consideration the extent that I rebelled against them, they set the template for my personality. My father had wanted to write; I became a writer.

When I sit down to write, I hear a voice in my head. Who sent me that voice? Did I fabricate it? If I did, I can't remember. In my case (*pace* those who insist the self is multivalent), that voice is singular. I don't hear *voices*; at this stage of life I'm too rigid and set in my ways, and so it tends to be the same damn voice jabbering on. All I know is that I keep listening for the voice to surprise me, say something out of the ordinary, provocative, mischievous, borderline dangerous. I go along in a civilized manner, generating reasonable discourse, and then I start to get bored. Hence, my love of contrariness. It's not that I've made up a contrarian or curmudgeonly persona, but that my physiological restlessness, my low tolerance for boredom, my neurotic antipathy to sentimentality all dictate that I throw in a dash of paradox, humorous chagrin, or spite. I wait to pounce with glee on some received truth. Meanwhile I record what the voice is telling me—not everything, I do refuse some inanities, but in the main I overwrite at this initial stage because I am taking down all that dictation, and so I end up having to cut back. It's really only at the editing stage that I can truthfully say I am constructing or fabricating an object, that I am "making a hat," as Stephen Sondheim says.

Now, the selection that occurs in the editing process has less to do with concocting a persona from scratch than with tweaking it—"it" being the familiar voice that I have been taking dictation from, lo these many years. Some factors that go into my suppressions and augmentations are the tonal and political values of the organ that commissioned the piece from me (or that I hope to solicit, if I am writing this on spec); the word-count or page limitations; and the social fear, on discovering I have written, perhaps inadvertently, something that could piss off a segment of the population. I like to take chances, but I am not an utter fool. In any event, even with the most pusillanimous corrections, I expect there will be readers who get angry at what I have written. Experience has taught me that there is no way I can shield myself in advance from giving offense to *someone*.

I hope these remarks will be accepted in the gentle spirit in which they were offered: as a mild demurral in the face of a new consensus. It's true that we make up our selves from moment to moment—as is readily apparent from observing any cocktail party or language arts convention—but it is also true that we have far less leeway in remaking ourselves and our personae on the page than we might first imagine.

# Research and Personal Writing

Those drawn to the writing of personal essays and memoirs are apt to discover the necessity to do some research. Sooner or later you run out of traumas and triumphs to recount; you have chewed up the tastiest limbs of your life story, and research becomes an alternative to further self-cannibalization. Even before that day arrives, you may find your memory can only take you so far: you need to go back to the old neighborhood and walk around, or talk to old-timers, or read up on local history, or pore through genealogical archives, housing deeds, census records.

There are other pluses to research, besides filling in the narrative gaps of autobiographical recollection with missing factual details. It can also bring a more general significance to your personal story. Research inspires curiosity, helps you break out of claustrophobic self-absorption and come to understand that you are not the only one who has passed down this road. You begin to see your experience as part of a larger pattern, be it sociological, historical, psychological, anthropological, cultural, political, or theological: these lenses can supply useful new perspectives to your private tale.

Let us say that you grew up in a relatively new suburb. It might not be a bad idea to examine what factors in American society fueled the postwar growth of suburbia: the Federal Highway Act, FHA loans, the utopian ethos of planned decentralization, the decay of urban downtowns, racism, white flight, and so on. (This is pretty much the approach that D. J. Waldie took in his *Holy Land: A Suburban Memoir.*) Or you witnessed your parents going through an ugly divorce: what insights can be gleaned from the writings of child psychiatrists about the ways that children adapt, or don't, to such situations? Or your parents were immigrants who spoke a language other than English at home, and you grew up torn between two cultures: what do anthropologists say about this problem? What do novelists and memoirists say about it? Or your father was a rocket engineer in the space program: how much astrophysics will it be necessary to learn and convey to the lay reader in order to put together a convincing account, as M. G. Lord did in *Astro Turf: The Private Life of Rocket Science?*

You may begin researching some technical field to provide a stronger answer to the question "Why should my little story count?"—and end up more interested in the area under study than in your personal narrative. You may find you are using your I-character more as a guide to help the reader through abstruse material than as the central focus. In other words, the proportion between self and world may shift in the process of researching. Or you may end up throwing out most of the research and just using a little bit as a spice to vary the prose palate. In most cases, however, research will assist you in conceptualizing more broadly the questions you would like to put to your experience.

Travel literature is one such area where the two approaches comfortably merge. The best travel writers, such as Robert Byron, Patrick Leigh Fermor, Ryszard Kapuscinski, Bruce Chatwin, or Kate Simon, employ their I-character to fetch adventures that can then be juicily related, while also doing extensive research on the countries through which they are traveling. Consider this passage from Chatwin's *In Patagonia*, and the way it weaves together personal experience and historical information:

> I left the Rio Negro and went on south to Port Madryn.
>
> A hundred and fifty-three Welsh colonists landed here off the brig *Mimosa* in 1863. They were poor people in search of a New Wales, refugees from cramped coal-mining valleys, from a failed Independence movement, and from Parliament's ban on Welsh in schools. Their leaders had combed the earth for a stretch of open country uncontaminated by Englishmen. They chose Patagonia for its absolute remoteness and foul climate; they did not want to get rich.
>
> The Argentine Government gave them land along the Chubut River. From Madryn it was a march of forty mules over the thorn desert. And when they did reach the valley, they had the impression that God, and not the Government, had given them the land. Port Madryn was a town of shabby concrete buildings, tin bungalows, tin warehouses and a wind-flattened garden. There was a cemetery of black cypresses and shiny black marble tombstones. The Calle Saint-Exupery was a reminder that the storm in *Vol de Nuit* was somewhere in these parts.
>
> I walked along the esplanade and looked out at the even line of cliffs spreading round the bay. The cliffs were a lighter grey than the grey of the sea and sky. The beach was grey and littered with dead penguins. Halfway along was a concrete monument in memory of the Welsh. It looked like the entrance to a bunker. Set into its sides were bronze reliefs representing Barbarism and Civilization.

Barbarism showed a group of Teheulche Indians, naked, with slabby back muscles in the Soviet style. The Welsh were on the side of Civilization—greybeards, young men with scythes, and big-breasted girls with babies.

Essayists and memoirists who are already scientists or doctors have an advantage over the rest of us, in that they can convey the wisdom and knowledge derived from their research with an easy authority. Hence, the appeal of such graceful literary savants as Loren Eiseley, Oliver Sacks, Stephen Jay Gould, Richard Selzer, and Lewis Thomas. In my next lifetime I hope to be a scientific scholar, but in the meantime, I give myself research assignments, sneaking off to the stacks whenever possible.

I was asked to contribute a personal essay for an anthology about the Book of Genesis, by picking a Bible story and ruminating on it. I chose to write about a pair of incidents when Abraham, fearing for his life when approaching the border of a potentially hostile people, passes off his wife Sarah as his sister. I could have stayed home and merely reflected on it, but instead I rushed off to the library to learn how the medieval rabbis and midrash writers and modern biblical scholars interpreted this seemingly cowardly act by a patriarch. What I discovered (some rationalized his act, others disapproved) formed the basis of the first part of my essay. Then I researched what Sigmund Freud and Karen Horney had to say about married couples devolving into sibling-like pairs, and that became the second panel. Finally I told the story of an incident that had occurred during my first marriage, when my wife and I were traveling through Morocco. The idea was that the personal vignette, which would have been inconclusive if recounted alone, would be enriched by the earlier perspectives provided by Rambam, Adin Steinsaltz, Freud, and Horney. I was looking to apply, through research, other lenses to my memoirist musings.

The main concern that students and emerging writers have about the research process is how to know when to stop. You begin poking around a complex new field—say, wine or rugs or nongovernment organizations in Africa—about which you know next to nothing; you realize that you could spend the rest of your life studying it; and you quickly become overwhelmed with its ever-expanding ramifications and think of giving up. Believe me, it does narrow eventually. After a few weeks at the library, on the Internet, or in the field, you notice that the sources are telling you something you already know, and you grasp the major schools of thought, their differences of opinion. Here the creative nonfiction writer can follow the journalists' lead. Being trained generalists—that is to say, quick studies who can leap opportunistically on intriguing vignettes and facts, give them a vivid twist, and forget the rest—veteran journalists know that they don't have to become specialists, they just have to absorb enough of the material under scrutiny this week or month to file an interesting story. When you are researching, what you are looking for, subconsciously or not, is the oddity that will spark your imagination—not necessarily the most important detail, but the one that will excite your love of paradox or sense of humor.

There comes a time when you feel you have done enough research for your modest purposes and can begin to write. Now you face a new dilemma: how to integrate the scholarly materials you have uncovered into your characteristic prose style? When I was writing *Waterfront*, I had to investigate a number of complex subjects, such as bridge engineering, marine biology, the anatomy of shipworms, public housing law. Each time I researched some new area, I was so impressed, so awed by the specialists' expertise, that I had a tendency to overquote them. I would think to myself, They know everything, I know nothing, how can I pretend to explain it when their language is so persuasive? This led to long, boring extracts, which my editor convinced me would have to go. I needed to paraphrase them somehow, put them in my own words, warm them with my stylistic breath. To convert this obdurate magma into something that sounded relatively essayistic, intimate, conversational, I had to call on every trick, irony, and witticism I could muster. At one point it meant lampooning the tone of a pedantic biologist; at another, playing up in a self-deprecating way my ignorance. I gave myself the challenge of writing the heroic but too-familiar saga of the construction of the Brooklyn Bridge in one long, Jamesian, convoluted sentence. I speeded up the geological cycle of the Ice Age like a silent comedy. No one commented on these devices, or perhaps even noticed them, but they helped reassure me I had put a personal stamp on this technical matter.

One of the best parts about researching is that it inspires in you an obligation to finish your writing project, if only to serve faithfully the scholarly materials to which you have become so attached. It is no longer all about *you*, but about them too, as though they had somehow become your offspring when you weren't watching. "Print me, Papa," beseech those index cards, those notepads, those Post-its.

# The Lyric Essay

Ambivalence being the essayist's nectar, I am happy to find some immediately in taking up the subject of the lyric essay. I mistrust the lyric essay; I welcome it; I don't know what it is.

First, mistrust. Since the nonlyric or shall we say the classical essay, against which the lyric essay is being posited by way of contrast, is an amazingly fluid, shape-shifting, language-engorging form, what is ostensibly so new about the lyric essay per se? Is it only historical ignorance of the classical essay's resourceful capacities that allow the champions of the lyric essay to proffer it as something novel? What does the lyric essay bring to the table? The cynic in me grumbles, Opacity, incoherence, preciosity. Or, more hopefully, an attention to the movements and undulations of language as a subject in itself; a replacement of the monaural, imperially ego-confident self, the I-character voice, with a more multivalent, realistically unstable, collaging system; a wedding of contemporary poetry and nonfiction.

In theory, it seems plausible and promising; in practice, thus far—with a few shimmering exceptions, such as the writing of John D'Agata, Eula Biss, Lia Purpura, Ander Monson, and Mary Cappello—more tantalizing than rewarding. In his letter soliciting contributions to an issue of *Seneca Review* specifically focusing on the lyrical essay, John D'Agata, the chief spokesman for the form, writes, "Over the past ten years, for instance, *Seneca Review* has had about a dozen essays chosen for *The Best American* anthology series. None of these texts however have been chosen as best American essays; all of them have been best American *poems*. On the first instance of this happening, the author of the essay that was chosen that year began her exasperated contributor's note with the line 'Well, I thought what I had written was an essay. . . .'"

While I can understand the frustration of these reclassified authors, often when I read examples of self-designated lyric essays, I do, to be honest, find them resembling a certain kind of experimental poetry that has proliferated over the past forty years, in the many little magazines around the New York School and the Language poets. There tends to be a reliance on structural, conceptual devices, such as lists or repeating word-phrases, a welcoming of stream-of-conscious, surrealist disjunctive leaps from line to line, and a suppression of mounting argument, replaced by circularity or trance, all of which link it to the kind of ethnopoetics that Jerome Rothenberg first allied with avant-garde poetics in his anthology *The Technicians of the Sacred*. In short, it is part of the larger rebellion against Western Enlightenment reason and linear, left-brain thinking.

As a proud descendant of the Enlightenment, I maintain that there is more room for mischief and circularity (see Diderot's *Jacques the Fatalist*) in this tradition than those who caricature it as rigid will allow. Even if this were not so, I would fear seeing rationality dismantled, given the alternatives. It seems to me that reasoning has long found a home in the essay, and I would not want to see it made unwelcome there.

I don't so much mind the lyric essay's eschewal of the banalities of the memoir piece, that staging of vignette about wound and redemption through compassionate insight. What bothers me more is the lyric essay's reluctance to let thought accrue to some purpose. Over the years I have come to feel that what interests me most in the classical personal essay, including the memoir essay, is the quality of rumination. It is the writer's thought, or consciousness, let us call it, that hooks me, not the ostensible plot. We all know by now that George Orwell is going to shoot that elephant, but what allows us to reread his essay each time with pleasure is the eloquent voicing of his subvocal hesitations, anticolonialist arguments, colonialist counterarguments, honestly admitted if lamentable prejudices, and peripheral sensory observations of the scene gathering around him. It is the same Orwell mind in action that draws me to his "Reflections on Gandhi" or "Politics and the English Language," which are not memoirist vignettes but ruminations that dare to follow out a line of reasoning to some conclusion.

If previously I saw the more amoeba-like personal essay as a way to evade the lawyerly, English Composition I setup of thesis, argument, example, and summary, I have come around to a healthier respect for using argument as a structural spine, however half-buried, which may explain part of my skepticism surrounding the lyric essay.

By the way, before we accept the lyric essay's claims that it is just trying to annex the free-floating, "difficult" freedom of the contemporary poem, we should remember that much fine contemporary poetry does employ argumentation, elaborate syntax, clarity, persuasion, and other rhetorical devices. So it is a matter of the essay's trying to become not simply more like poetry, but like one kind of poetry.

When creative writing students tell me that they want to investigate and even specialize in lyric essays, I worry, partly because I doubt my own capacity to guide them well in these (for me) largely uncharted waters, but also because it is invariably just those students who have the dreamiest, least-grounded styles, who have never developed a strong narrative voice and a firm grasp of argumentation—the two are often interrelated—who ask for this dispensation. It seems to me they are angling for a license for their dreamy vagueness, which will allow them to dither on "lyrically," trying the patience of most readers. Not that the reader should not be frustrated from time to time, but I prefer that these provocations arise from suspenseful rigor rather than formlessness. A digression properly placed can be a marvelous bridge to deepening thought; a piece made entirely of digressions is apt to stay on the surface.

Some of my doubts about the lyric essay stem from petty rivalry; I wouldn't want you to think I was only being high-minded about these matters. If my graduate students are being lured away to the lyrical essay, it makes me jealous, particularly since John D'Agata is younger and cuter than I am. All these territorial squabbles are pathetic.

Once, I was kindly asked by Mr. D'Agata to contribute to a special *Seneca Review* issue on the lyrical essay. Not knowing what exactly a lyrical essay was, but wanting as a colleague to oblige and, more important, not be left behind by the passing parade, I went to my folder of dead poems—these were efforts from my poetry-writing days that had not quite worked out—and retyped a number of them as prose by obliterating the line breaks. The result was a collage of fragments that apparently was good enough to qualify for publication. I had faked it and not gotten caught. On the other hand, I noticed I was not asked to contribute to Mr. D'Agata's groundbreaking anthology *The Next New Essay*. It made me bitter to think I had been cast aside, to lurk back with the shades of the Old Essayists, the ones not hip enough or postmodernist enough. Then again, I knew in my heart I was not a lyric essayist, so where did I get off complaining that I'd been excluded from their camp?

I think we essayists are all looking for ways to make our efforts as open, capacious, and inviting of heterogeneous materials as possible, while still pressing them into reasonably elegant formal structures that will embody and reinforce their meanings. The essay, be it lyrical or ruminative, New Wave or traditional, enjoys a remarkable potential freedom today—partly because it has such a tenuous relationship with the larger commercial culture. So I salute lyric essayists everywhere as my brethren, or maybe I should say my half siblings, in this financially impractical, aesthetically quixotic venture. Long may we lyricize and essay.

# The Personal Essay in the
# Age of Facebook

We humans are always trying to sneak a peak ahead at the effects that new technologies might be having on us, and it is never fruitful to do so, any more than a patient under the knife while receiving anesthesia can analyze the situation, or the hapless victim of floodwaters being swept away, or, perhaps to use a more apt comparison, the dodo bird unwittingly undergoing Darwinian evolution. So now we personal essayists are being asked to examine our plight and to prognosticate. Can we stand up to the onslaught of Facebook and Twitter? Can we co-opt the dark powers they have set in motion and use them to prolong our own precarious existence? Do I know the answers to these questions? Of course not. But as one of the chief dodos, I have a certain proprietary interest in the personal essay, which I hope gives me the right to meander on the subject for a few pages.

First I would like to say that part of what drew me initially to the personal essay was that it was an underutilized genre, generally neglected both by the academy and commercial publishers. It flew under the radar, giving its practitioners more freedom to go anywhere they wanted. It may have become a tad more popular or conspicuous in the last twenty years, but let us not get carried away: those gifted personal essayists who are trying to get their first collections published still face daunting odds. All this I offer by way of assurance: the personal essay is not headed for a great fall in the Facebook Age, because it never rose very high to begin with. Such a minority taste, involving small numbers of occult alchemical practitioners and even smaller numbers of devoted readers, has nothing to fear from mass communication techniques promoting interchange, above all, between teenagers insecure about their popularity, such as Facebook or Myspace. We are like druids to them; even the young ones among us appear to them as fuddy-duddies; they ignore us and we can return the favor.

The true personal essayist is not only antiquated but an antiquarian, who gladly draws on and plays with the historical traditions of the form. It has been that way ever since Montaigne quoted and jousted with the ancients, Seneca, Plutarch, and Cicero, or Lamb invoked in his mannered prose the shades of Thomas Browne, Robert Burton, and the Duchess of Newcastle. Personal essayists are in a conversation with their ancestors, trying both to renovate the same subjects, such as friendship and manners, while paying homage to their dead betters with sly winks toward the past. There will always be cultivated readers who respond to these historical palimpsests, this archaeological layering of prose, the pleasurable ironies of archaic diction or complex syntax.

We frequently make the error of believing in aesthetic progress, as though artistic expression were required to follow an agenda that pointed in only one direction. So modernism ostensibly taught us that, after Pound, there was no going back to

Swinburne, and after Hemingway, no possible return to Henry James. But see what has happened to the contemporary prose sentence. Many confidently assumed that the telegraph and typewriter had influenced Hemingway, leading to a more stripped-down sentence, a cutting away of clausal ornamentation, and the post-Hemingway sentence became even more streamlined in the hands of Raymond Carver and the other minimalists. It looked as though all prose sentences were going in the direction of the tweet, with its limited number of characters. Then along came David Foster Wallace, and his mighty confusions and perplexities, and Nicholson Baker, piling clause on clause, and Rick Moody's postmodernist flourishes, not to mention foreign writers such as W. G. Sebald, Thomas Bernhard, Milan Kundera, Roberto Bolaño, José Saramago, Javier Marías, all of whom took the sentence in ever more baroque directions. They were acting out of their own individual obstinacy and literary learning, and perhaps also responding to an unconscious taste on the part of the culture for more variety and a denser ideational complexity. Because some thoughts cannot be expressed in the Strunk and White, keep-it-simple-and-clear recipe, they require a more sinuous, self-reflective, devious syntax.

All this is good news for the personal essay, so dependent on reflection, so free to tell as well as show. And it is no surprise that many of the authors I just mentioned have been as drawn to the essay as they were to the novel; in a sense, their chief innovation was to smuggle into fiction the voice of the ruminative personal essayist. If they could do it—resist the siren song of the bare, text-message sentence—and be so successful in the process, the rest of us should take heart. In short, there is more life in the language of prose than just Twitter's 140 characters and Facebook's emoticons.

But I do not want to represent Facebook as some sort of opponent to the personal essay when it could very well be an ally. The accusation that Facebook encourages its users to wallow in self-absorption and narcissism has also been frequently leveled at the personal essay and the memoir in the last twenty years. And it is not automatically true in either case. Any first attempt at self-definition is a useful step on the way to effective autobiographical writing, which can keep the ego in perspective. The same thing is true for blogs: even as we speak, there are sharply written, well-shaped, self-aware blogs on the Internet, alongside self-indulgent verbal diarrhea. With the paucity of publishing outlets for personal essays, we should welcome the bloggers or Facebook writers who are trying out their ideas without necessarily getting paid for them. (Some of them have already figured out a way to get paid, the lucky devils.) Eventually, quality will sort itself out: that is already happening to some extent.

What of our fears that the new technologies are causing the younger generation to mutate into cell phone–transfixed or BlackBerry-addicted zombies? I am certainly as annoyed as the next person when I have to get out of the way of someone crossing the street who has not bothered to look up from his iPhone, just as I am bothered when I have to listen to a pretty young woman laughing on the cell phone when I could have been flirtatiously catching her eye. But I am not sure I agree with those who warn that a tragic atrophying of our ability to notice the physical world is taking place. Even before the invention of cell phones, most people (myself included) failed to notice ninety-five percent of what was going on around them. Henry James may have famously advised the prospective writer to be someone on whom nothing is lost, but I rather think that even the best writers select out most of what is going on in their daily environments and work with only those details that stubbornly stick to their brainpans.

Future personal essayists, brought up on Facebook, will undoubtedly notice different details from those we did; in any case, they will have no shortage of things to notice.

And so the personal essay will continue—maybe not thrive, but persist. We are like bedbugs, hard to see, harder to kill off, sucking at the blood of the larger culture. Which is it to be, personal essayists: dodo bird or bedbug?

# II.

## STUDIES OF
## PRACTITIONERS

# Lamb's *Essays of Elia*

T*he Essays of Elia*, by Charles Lamb, is one of the classics of English prose, and a cornerstone of the personal essay tradition. All personal essayists worth their salt owe a huge debt to this generous and generative collection, whether they know it or not; all apprentice essayists who would strive to make headway in the form should read it. If you read Lamb, in any case, it is not a chore but a delicious stylistic treat, for he is one of those writers who wants to bring pleasure to his readers and usually will—provided you commit your attention and surrender to the terms by which he offers himself.

Having said that, I must backpedal and acknowledge that *The Essays of Elia* is not only an essential text but a near-buried treasure, an all-but-lost masterpiece in our contemporary culture, one that stands in periodic danger of going out of print and so must be rescued periodically by heroic preservationists. Why has so good and entertaining a classic become so endangered? I would guess that it has something to do with our altered reading habits, which have brought a preference for stark, simply digested prose and a resistance to densely packed, complex sentences; with the abundance of references Lamb makes that may seem dated or bewildering to today's reader; and finally, with his sheer *strangeness*, which raises the question of authorial intent. For Lamb is not your Everyman, not your average Joe, but a very precisely and peculiarly ordered sensibility, whose acute sense of his difference from other people was both a source of strength and loneliness. In highlighting those eccentricities, he drew out of himself an unforgettable three-dimensional character.

It is a truism of autobiographical writing that to render your own character on the page honestly, you must be able to stand back and look at yourself objectively, in the third person, as it were. No one can do it completely, but at least the effort must be made. The way Lamb chose was by inventing a persona or mask, Elia, who would speak for him. Elia allowed him to have it both ways: to be shockingly honest while pretending that his narrator was a fiction, and to gain a little playful distance for self-examination. By and large, Elia *is* Lamb, temperamentally speaking, and their résumés and circumstances have very much in common, but there are also significant autobiographical omissions from the record. (All autobiographical first persons are highly selective and therefore distorting representations of their owners, even when they do not bother, as Lamb did, to employ an alter ego or pen name.) And there are mischievous alterations, as when Elia takes issue with Charles Lamb's portrait of the boys' school they both attended, Christ's Hospital. Elia twits Lamb for having it easy and not seeing the different class treatment meted out for boys less fortunate. In general, Elia is Lamb minus the latter's social stature and literary achievement.

Lamb's first-person narrator loses no opportunity in belittling himself, turning his inabilities or limitations into a sort of reverse essayistic capital: he has no musical ear, is lazy, at times immature, an unsystematic reader who keeps going back to the same dusty books. He defines himself as out of step with his times, rooted in the past, shirking the responsibilities of adulthood, and clinging to childish things. "I am naturally, beforehand, shy of novelties; new books, new faces, new years,—from some mental twist which makes it difficult in me to face the prospective," he writes in one of his most revealing essays, "New Year's Eve," and goes on to say,

That I am fond of indulging, beyond a hope of sympathy, in such retrospection, may be the symptom of some sickly idiosyncrasy. Or is it owing to another cause; simply, that being without wife or family, I have not learned to project myself enough out of myself; and having no offspring of my own to dally with, I turn back upon memory, and adopt my own early idea [of himself as a child], as my heir and favourite? If these speculations seem fantastical to thee—(a busy man, perchance), if I tread out of the way of thy sympathy, and am singularly-conceited only, I retire, impenetrable to ridicule, under the phantom cloud of Elia.

Here we have an introspective tone that predicts and has more in common with those crabbed, divided antiheroes such as Dostoevsky's Underground Man or Svevo's Zeno than with the earlier, amiably capable eighteenth-century protagonists of Fielding. Indeed, one could make the case that Lamb/Elia is one of the first truly modern characters to appear on the literary stage. Here too we have that cheeky reply of the Superfluous Man to the "busy" man of affairs, and a clear statement of the defensive use Lamb made of Elia. It was a familiar strategy of early personal essayists to ward off potential criticisms of conceit and egotism (or, as we would say today, narcissism) by portraying themselves as fundamentally weak, powerless, marginal—more to be indulged than feared. Lamb took this basic figure of the idling, spectator bachelor (used by Dr. Johnson, Addison and Steele, Washington Irving, and others) and fleshed it out into a full-fledged modern neurotic. He had the quintessential personal essayist's ability to see his own personality as problematic, and to dramatize the resulting tensions. Not that he had to go very far: Lamb's past was both idyllic and a minefield, as we can see by reviewing the main events of his life.

Charles Lamb (1775–1834) was born in a quiet, cloistered section of buildings in London called the Temple, connected to the law courts. His father, John Lamb, was a clerk and servant, who married Elizabeth Field, a housekeeper's daughter. They had seven children, three of whom survived: Charles, the youngest; his ten years' older sister, Mary, who helped raise Charles; and the oldest brother, John. Lamb went to Christ's Hospital on a scholarship and befriended there the brilliant future poet Samuel Taylor Coleridge. But because of his family's worsening financial circumstances, Charles was forced to quit school and go to work at fourteen as a clerk at the South-Sea House. A few years later he switched to the East India House, where he clerked for the rest of his working life.

At the age of twenty, Lamb witnessed a horrific family tragedy: his beloved sister Mary, under a great nervous strain from having to attend to her ailing parents and run the household while taking in needlework, stabbed their mother to death and wounded their father. Here is how Charles described the tragedy in a September 27, 1796, letter to Coleridge: "I will only give you the outlines:—My poor dear, dearest sister, in a fit of insanity, has been the death of her mother. I was at hand only time enough to snatch the knife out of her grasp. She is at present in a madhouse, from whence I fear she must be moved to a hospital. God has preserved to me my senses—I eat, and drink, and sleep, and have my judgment, I believe, very sound." Mary was spared prison by the courts and remanded to the custody of her younger brother, who took care of her (as she did him) for the rest of their lives. They were very close and collaborated on several writing projects, including the children's classic *Tales from Shakespeare*. Periodically Mary would suffer relapses and have to be readmitted to the madhouse; a friend reported how he "met the brother and sister on one such occasion, walking hand in hand across the fields to the old asylum, both bathed in tears." In general, however, his sister provided a calm domestic stability that allowed Charles to persist at his tedious clerical job and hone his craft after hours as a writer.

Lamb remained a bachelor; his one professed love had been for a blonde with blue eyes, Alice W——, who turned him down and married an undertaker, but we have no idea to what degree this early "broken heart" experience genuinely inhibited him from further romances or was merely a prankish literary device. Perhaps both. Certainly his emotional life remained centered on his sister Mary, and his appetite for books, plays, friendships, and the spectacle of London.

Lamb had a great zest for theater and began writing impressive drama criticism (*Specimens of English Dramatic Poets*). His own attempts at playwriting failed; with characteristic self-mockery, he joined the crowd who hooted at the premiere of his lame farce *Mr. H——* (about a gentleman, ashamed because his name is Hogsflesh, who tries to cover up the fact at all costs). He had more success moonlighting as a journalist, supplying jokes and one-paragraph squibs for the newspapers. In 1820, at age forty-five, he began writing the pieces that would eventually become *The Essays of Elia* for *London Magazine* (which also published such eminent writers as William Hazlitt, John Keats, and Thomas

De Quincey). He took the name Elia from an Italian clerk he had known as a boy at the South-Sea House. This lightly fictionalizing device allowed him to transform Mary into "Cousin Bridget," who pops up frequently in these essays, and to paint a rather more barbed portrait of his selfish older brother John, who becomes a cousin, "James Elia." Nowhere is the deliberate confusion between author and persona more wrenching than in the heartbreaking conclusion of "Dream Children," written shortly after his brother John's death. Elia snaps out of his reverie and finds himself "quietly seated in my bachelor arm-chair, where I had fallen asleep, with the faithful Bridget unchanged by my side—but John L. (or James Elia) was no more." By using both names, it is as if the author cannot make up his mind whether to disguise or name the loss.

Curiously, though he was not averse to handling painful subjects, Lamb never wrote about his mother's murder; perhaps it was too gaudy and horrific to suit his whimsical, lapidary style. William Carlos Williams says in a poem about René Char that he must have had a very hard life, to write so tenderly about flowers. One feels in Lamb's gentle embrace of everyday customs and paradoxes a similar motive: an obstinate refusal to engage with the violent and apocalyptic, a refusal that may very well have had its roots in that traumatic event. On the other hand, Lamb's gift for humor may have been so temperamentally predetermined and ingrained that no amount of personal tragedy could have deterred him from expressing it.

Lamb is a great comic writer. He can bring a smile to your lips by the spin he puts on a single word. He loves to parody the stiffness of scholarly writing by using a ridiculously Latinate term for a simple object, as when he describes the substance near the crackling in "A Dissertation on Roast Pig" as "the adhesive oleaginous—O call it not fat!" There is that same euphemistic, mock-fastidious concern for naming things in "The South-Sea House" when he stops short of calling a clerk cowardly: "With all this there was about him a sort of timidity (his few enemies used to give it a worse name)—a something which, in reverence to the dead, we will place, if you please, a little on this side of the heroic."

Sometimes the language takes off seemingly on its own. Here is the opening of "A Chapter on Ears":

> I have no ear.
>
> Mistake me not, Reader—nor imagine that I am by nature destitute of those exterior twin appendages, hanging ornaments, and (architecturally speaking) handsome volutes to the human capital. Better my mother had never borne me.—I am, I think, rather delicately than copiously provided with those conduits; and I feel no disposition to envy the mule for his plenty, or the mole for her exactness, in those ingenious labyrinthine inlets—those indispensable side-intelligencers.

He sounds drunk on language. He's on a tear. Some of today's readers may miss the humor, not realizing that all this ornate verbiage, and the "thees" and "thous," were considered quaint and old-fashioned even when Lamb wrote. He loved archaic, mildewed vocabulary, which he used with solemn mockery—as he did puns, absurd pileups of metaphors, and buffoonish catalogues. He fashioned his style on English Renaissance prose writers such as Sir Thomas Browne, Robert Burton, and Sir William Temple, who were encyclopedically learned but of interest mainly to antiquarian booksellers, even in Lamb's day. Lamb took that style and retooled it into a kind of inspired nonsense. With Lawrence Sterne, he helped to initiate that tradition of bookish parody we now associate with postmodernism.

Lamb has a genius for elaboration, for drawing out a sly idea into a paragraph that sets off a chain reaction of laughs. In "New Year's Eve," he tantalizes the reader with a confession of his faults, which keeps being frustrated by the interruptions of asterisks: "If I know aught of myself, no one whose mind is introspective— and mine is painfully so—can have a less respect for his present identity than I have for the man Elia. I know him to be light, and vain, and humoursome; a notorious ***; addicted to ***; averse from counsel, neither taking it, nor offering it;—*** besides; a stammering buffoon; what you will; lay it on, and spare not; I sub-scribe to it all, and much more. . . ." There are echoes of Shake-speare's Falstaff in his buffoonery.

Some of Lamb's humor is not linguistic so much as psycho-logical.

A key notion of Lamb's about human character, perhaps derived from his lifelong fascination with the theater, is that people are actors. Not only does he analyze the styles of famous actors of his time in the collection's three concluding essays, but he sees everyday life, and particularly the London streets, as a stage. Lamb brings on the clerks, in his essay "The South-Sea House," one by one as though they are the second-string mem-bers of a repertory troupe. In the midst of describing one particu-lar clerk, he remarks parenthetically, "He is the true actor, who, whether his part be a prince or a peasant, must act it with like intensity. With Tipp form was everything. His life was formal. His actions seemed ruled with a ruler." He concludes his brilliant "Complaint of the Decay of Beggars in the Metropolis" with the advice *"give and ask no questions."* What if a beggar is lying when he tells you he has seven children to support? "Rake not into the bowels of unwelcome truth to save a halfpenny. It is good to believe him. If he be not all that he pretendeth, give, and under a personate father of a family, think (if thou pleasest) that thou hast relieved an indigent bachelor. When they come with their counterfeit looks and mumping tones, think them players. You pay your money to see a comedian feign these things."

Again and again, Lamb's is the voice of compassionate wisdom, offering sympathy to those left out of the imperial feast: the beggars, the old women, the child chimney sweeps. If he is harder on the comfortable, solid, bourgeois family man, it is because he cannot tolerate hypocrisy or smugness. Much of the satire that he directs toward the manners and mores of his day issues from this reflex. In "Grace before Meat," he finds the custom of thanking the Creator for a bountiful meal, when so many others go hungry, an exercise in self-congratulation. In "Modern Gallantry," he says he will believe the claims that we are becoming more chivalric than our ancestors when we stop whipping or hanging women, or when a young gentleman gives up his seat for a poor old apple-woman, instead of for a pretty girl of his own social station. "Lastly, I shall begin to believe that there is some such principle influencing our conduct, when more than one-half of the drudgery and coarse servitude of the world shall cease to be performed by women."

At such moments Lamb begins to sound like a radical. He was not. While living in a time of revolutions, he stayed away from politics, for the most part, but he was observant, particularly to widening imbalances between the haves and the have-nots. Even his comic essay "A Bachelor's Complaint of the Behavior of Married People" registers, from the viewpoint of the love-starved outsider, how insulting and cruel can be the unconsciously smug spectacle of family life.

Lamb was much more celebrated for his tenderness toward

his subjects ("Saint Charles," Thackeray called him) than his bite, but he did have teeth and was not afraid to bare them. In a book that has such triumphs of fondness as "The Praise of Chimney-Sweepers" or "The Old Benchers of the Inner Temple," it is almost startling to come upon the essay "Imperfect Sympathies," wherein Lamb characterizes himself as a "bundle of prejudices." Examining his resistance to spending much time with Scotsmen, Jews, Negroes, or Quakers, he crosses our own line of political correctness more than once. But you have to hand it to him, Lamb was not a hypocrite, and there is something refreshingly honest about his seeking to define the limits of his sympathies, the better to refine his aspirations toward compassion.

Lamb had quite a range of narrative manner and employed a battery of structural devices: there is the memoir of place and the parade of characters in "The South-Sea House"; the sustained character portrait of a person with a one-track mind in "Mrs. Battle's Opinions on Whist"; the dividing up of humanity into two camps, the late and the punctual, the borrowers and the lenders, in "The Two Races of Man"; the hilariously straight-faced, faux-scholarly folk tale of "A Dissertation on Roast Pig," which switches in the last third to a culinary encomium to Lamb's favorite dish; "New Year's Eve," which revolves from a lighthearted analysis of a holiday to a somber meditation on death, only to kick up its heels in the end; the miraculous, soap-bubble reverie of "Dream Children," with its final settling back to earth. Just when you think he is all charm and whimsical imagination, you come across an essay like "The Old and New Schoolteacher," with its deeply realistic insights about vocation and life's disappointments. "My First Play" seems intended to move classically from enchantment to disenchantment (the child's loss of stage illusion), but then it surprises us by recouping enchantment through the more sophisticated means of connoisseurship. A Lamb essay may alter its course several times, like a broken-field runner, before coming to a stop—and you never know where ahead of time.

He followed his thoughts, trusting to their rambles here and there, rather like his continental predecessor in the essay, Montaigne. In this respect, he differed from his friend and chief contemporary rival as England's supreme essayist, William Hazlitt, whose philosophical training led to a more tenacious pursuit of argument. Then again, the Romantic Hazlitt quickly got hot under the collar, broke with friends, and made enemies quickly, whereas Lamb tended to be tolerant, skeptical, and amused by difference. In company, Lamb's gifts for wit and sociability were much prized. He stammered, which took the sting off some of his witticisms. (One of my favorites occurred at his clerical job. Upbraided for showing up frequently late to work, Lamb offered to make up for it by leaving early.)

*The Essays of Elia* was immediately appreciated when it appeared, and brought Lamb in middle age a modest amount of gratifying celebrity. His employers also gave him a retirement pension, allowing him to enjoy a brief few years' leisure. He wrote a second set, called *The Last Essays of Elia*, which included a half-dozen gems—"The Convalescent," "Old China," "The Superannuated Man," "Poor Relations," "Blakesmoor in H——shire," "Detached Thoughts on Books and Reading"—though there was, to be honest, an overall decline in quality. Lamb himself acknowledged it in the remarkable Preface to the second volume, "by a friend of the late Elia." There he says, "To say truth, it is time he were gone. The humor of the thing, if ever there was much in it, was pretty well exhausted; and two years' and a half existence has been a tolerable duration for a phantom."

He then goes on to anatomize the weaknesses in "my late friend's writings," which include "a self-pleasing quaintness," an "affected array of antique modes," an overuse of "that dangerous figure—irony," and a careless, scattershot manner of composition. As if this were not bad enough, Lamb zeroes in on Elia's (and his own) character flaws, saying with astuteness, "He was too much of the boy-man. The *toga virilis* never sate gracefully on his shoulders. The impressions of infancy had burnt into him, and he resented the impertinences of manhood." It is hard to imagine a male writer of our day making a similar confession of insufficient virility.

Charles Lamb may never have accepted the rigid terms of manhood or adulthood that English society proposed for him, but if the courage to examine oneself thoroughly and achieve a laughing perspective on one's foibles is a plausible definition of achieving maturity (and I think it is), then he was quite a man.

# Hazlitt on Hating

First cousin to the contrarian essay that sets up in opposition to a presumed good (such as Joyce Carol Oates's "Against Nature," Witold Gombrowicz's "Against Poetry" or Laura Kipnis's *Against Love*) is the devil's advocate essay that seeks to defend an ostensible vice or distasteful condition. Take any negative trait to which aversion might be the expected response and imagine a celebration of its hidden value: "The Solace of Despair," say, "The Joys of Envy," or "The Divinity of Cigarettes." Perhaps the greatest of such exercises in topsy-turvyism is William Hazlitt's "On the Pleasure of Hating." Hazlitt (1778–1830) was already regarded as a nervy, compulsively readable essayist-critic (many today rank him among the greatest stylists in the English language) when he took this provocative position in his 1826 collection, *The Plain Speaker*.

We are all taught from earliest childhood that hating is a bad thing. The trick of Hazlitt's essay is he does not *advocate* for hatred; he observes its ubiquitous presence in our lives and tries to account for that fact. In short, the essay, I would argue, is not mean-spirited or hateful in itself, but *about* hatred. Hazlitt is a writer of such fluency, with his long unbroken paragraphs, active verbs, ready examples, fresh metaphors, and swift transitions, that the essay can feel like a single onrush, a great gush of rhetorical assertion. Let us slow it down, however, to try and understand how it works, and also how it mutates along the way.

The essay begins by invoking the image of the spider as a creature that, in spite of our knowing that it serves a useful function in the great scheme of things, most of us instinctively revile. The spider's appearance is described: "He runs with heedless, hurried haste, he hobbles awkwardly towards me, he stops—he sees the giant shadow before him, and, at a loss whether to retreat or proceed, meditates his huge foe—but as I do not start up or seize upon the struggling caitiff, as he would upon a helpless fly within his toils, he takes heart and ventures on, with mingled cunning, impudence and fear." Hazlitt's syntax mimics the spider's hesitant, stutter-step movements; his tone is detached, curious, almost sympathetic, similar in spirit to Virginia Woolf's observations of the moth in her "Death of a Moth" piece a hundred years later. He then remarks, "A child, a woman, a clown, or a moralist a century ago, would have crushed the little reptile to death—my philosophy has got beyond that—I bear the creature no ill will, but still I hate the very sight of it." We will pass over Hazlitt's taxonomical error: the point is that he is confessing to a murderous impulse, which he holds in check. Civilization has arrived at a stage of sufficient benevolence, he argues, that it is not necessary to enact violence against everything that repels us, but it has not yet reached a point where we can overcome our initial primitive response to the spider, "a sort of mystic horror and superficial loathing. It will ask another hundred years of fine writing and hard thinking to cure us of the prejudice."

Hazlitt, a political progressive, is here mocking himself and the educated classes for their belief in progress and reason. Like Montaigne, his forerunner, he remains skeptical of the claims of rationality. Pre-Darwin, he is saying that we still have the instinctual makeup of apes and cavemen. Note, too, the term "prejudice." Despite the consensus of opprobrium attached to that word today, I take it as a given that personal essayists must examine their prejudices and instinctual aversions as starting points for any honest analysis of their characters and views. Ralph Waldo Emerson, in a notebook entry for October 14, 1834, wrote, "Every involuntary repulsion that arises in your mind give heed unto. It is the surface of a central truth."

The "central truth" that Hazlitt explores in the next long (three-page!) paragraph is that hatred seems to provide an essential flavoring, or spice, that we need in order to keep life from becoming intolerably bland. Again, note the tone of the disinterested scientist, when he says "the more we look into it" or posits a series of theoretical questions without answering them: he is not championing hatred; he is trying to explain why it has had such a long run:

> Nature seems (the more we look into it) made up of antipathies: without something to hate, we should lose the very spring of thought and action. Life would turn to a stagnant pool, were it not ruffled by the jarring interests, the unruly passions of men. The white streak in our own fortunes is brightened (or just rendered visible) by making all round it as dark as possible, so the rainbow paints its form upon the cloud. Is it pride? Is it envy? Is it force of contrast? Is it weakness or malice? But so it is, that there is a secret affinity, a *hankering* after evil in the human mind, and that it takes a perverse, but fortunate delight in mischief, since it is a never-failing source of satisfaction. Pure good soon grows insipid, wants variety and spirit. Pain is a bitter-sweet which never surfeits. Love turns,

with a little indulgence, to indifference and disgust: hatred alone is immortal.

We can interpret this passage as representing both Hazlitt's underlying psychology of human behavior and his aesthetics. From the psychological standpoint, he seems to be saying that the happiness we seek is not arrived at through a cessation in tension but through the proper amount of stimulation, which must be endlessly recalibrated. We go through life like an electromagnetic needle nervously agitating between the undesirable poles of alpha-flat zombie and tortured suffering, trying to find the right voltage of bracingly vivifying pleasure/pain in the middle. Aesthetically, he could have been speaking about literature, voicing those by-now-familiar prescriptions that every story must have conflict, that an essay cannot be allowed to slip into static mode, and that wholesome pieties or purely virtuous characters quickly cloy.

With his essayist's gift for elaboration, he goes on to give many illustrations of the pain-craving principle: men rush to witness executions or fires, children kill flies for sport, the masses are whipped up by religious schisms and patriotic disputes to fight bloody wars, local feuds are extended generation after generation, witches are burned at the stake, and other ghastly superstitions persist.

There is a funny moment when he reverts to the idea that we are beasts at heart: "The wild beast resumes its sway within us, we feel like hunting-animals, and as the hound starts in his sleep and rushes on the chase in fancy, the heart rouses itself in its native lair, and utters a wild cry of joy, at being restored once more to freedom and lawless, unrestrained impulses. Every one has his full swing, or goes to the Devil his own way. Here are no Jeremy Bentham Panopticons . . . no more long calculations of self-interest." Hazlitt is making fun of utilitarian philosophers such as Bentham who saw humanity as governed by a rational calculus of self-interest. This was, incidentally, the very same utilitarianism that Dostoevsky's narrator in *Notes from Underground* took exception to, decades later, and his antidote would be quite similar to Hazlitt's: the perversity of spite. Both authors saw man as a creature needing to feel free, even if by intentionally spiting one's own self-interests.

Hazlitt is appropriately identified with the English Romantic literary movement, as the nonfiction prose counterpart of poets Keats, Shelley, Wordsworth, and Byron; witness his frequent recourse to terms such as "passion" and "feeling," as well as his eagerness to locate behavior in subjectivity. If you read Hazlitt side by side with Samuel Johnson, there is no question that the balanced periodicity of Johnson's English prose has undergone a rash transformation in Hazlitt's hands; the sentences have become wilder, more energetic, jerky, with dashes and sudden stops. There is a new appetite for the grotesque and for unappeasable neurotic discontent, alongside impatience with stoicism or social consensus. The Augustan Age has in effect yielded to the Romantic. At the same time, Hazlitt had originally wanted to be a philosopher and had a reserved but immense respect for Johnson, so one can still find orderly argumentation in Hazlitt, underneath the sword thrusts. And he is still a child of the Enlightenment, furthering the line of Voltaire, Diderot, Jefferson, who sought to dispel superstition and bigotry. Though he uses the pronoun "we" throughout the lengthy inventory of man's proclivity for pain (perhaps to create a bond between essayist and reader, or to not appear a superior scold), the fact remains that Hazlitt would not have partaken of these particular follies. *He* did not chase after executions, persecute witches, or fight wars for or against the pope.

To recap the pronominal strategy of the essay so far: on the opening page Hazlitt employs the first person pronoun, but his "I" is merely an unspecific surrogate for the general reader—a way of getting his audience to acknowledge their own instinctual antipathies. The next three pages, executed in one long paragraph, switch to first-person plural and roam broadly over history, nationalism, religion, and superstition, with examples that show how ridiculous and destructive humanity can be (though not Hazlitt himself, nor presumably his readers, the cultivated liberals apt to buy a collection such as *The Plain Speaker*). Then a space break comes, and with it a change in perspective, a deepening intimacy. From this point on (after a brief summation of the spleen generated by religion and patriotism), Hazlitt turns more personal, shifts his focus from public to private life, and gives us much more of his experience as an idiosyncratic, singular, literary man. As well, he now admits to his complicity in the kind of painful antipathies he is talking about. The tonal shift occurs with the memorable, characteristically paratactic line, which lays out the program for what is to follow: "We hate old friends: we hate old books: we hate old opinions; and at last we come to hate ourselves."

I don't think it's a coincidence that the first item mentioned in this list is "old friends." The essay now shifts to ruminating on the fragility of friendship, and this becomes its central matter. Why do some friendships come to an end, peter out, lose their savor, fail to nourish after a while? Sexual love is famously transient, but there is at least the consolation that everyone knows it to be so; whereas friendships arouse the almost utopian expectation that, barring some foolish quarrel, two like-minded people should be able to maintain amicable relations for a lifetime. When this does not happen, when a friendship fizzles out, the pain and grief that result may leave keener wounds, or certainly a graver perplexity, than the death of a love affair, because it is so unexpected.

"I have observed that few of those, whom I have formerly known most intimate, continue on the same friendly footing, or combine the steadiness with the warmth of attachment. I have been acquainted with two or three knots of inseparable companions who saw each other 'six days in the week,' that have broken up and dispersed. I have quarreled with almost all my old friends, (they might say this is owing to my bad temper, but) they have also quarreled with one another." Hazlitt, knowing his reputation for being hotheaded, here anticipates the contemporary reader's objection in order to deflect it. He goes on to speak about the circle that gathered around his fellow essayist and periodic friend Charles Lamb: "What is become of 'that set of whist-players,' celebrated by Elia . . . ? They are scattered, like last year's snow. Some of them are dead—or gone to live at a distance—or pass one another in the street like strangers; or if they stop to speak, do it coolly and try to *cut* one another as soon as possible." Why is this so? How did this state of affairs come about? Hazlitt has a theory (though he would not have used that word). In part, it is an extension of what he said earlier about the need for ever-new stimulation in human relations, but another part, perhaps the more original, has it that it is very difficult to find a true friend who is exactly at one's level, and having done so, to sustain this parity over time. Should there arise the least inequality in social status, intellectual power, money, or family happiness, a struggle for dominance and subsequent alienation will likely ensue.

Here is how Hazlitt describes it:

Old friendships are like meats served up repeatedly, cold, comfortless and distasteful. The stomach turns against them. Either constant intercourse and familiarity breed weariness and contempt; or if we meet again after an interval of absence, we appear no longer the same. One is too wise, another too foolish for us; and we wonder we did not find this out before. We are disconcerted and kept in a state of continual alarm by the wit of one, or tired to death of the dullness of another. The *good things* of the first (besides leaving stings behind them) by repetition grow stale, and lose their startling effect; and the insipidity of the last becomes intolerable. The most amusing or instructive companion is at best like a favorite volume, that we wish after a time to *lay upon the shelf;* but as our friends are not willing to be laid there, this produces a misunderstanding and ill-blood between us.

Friendship has long been a common topic among philosophers and essayists, going back to Aristotle and Cicero and extending through Montaigne, but I know no one else who wrote about its problematic aspects before with Hazlitt's unsentimental honesty. His metaphors portray friendship as a commodity with a shelf life: a victual ("meat") to gobble down, or "a favorite volume" to peruse until overfamiliarity sets in. It's true that writer friends often do approach each other as walking books and exult whenever the friend's conversation jolts them into new ideas, though later they can grow disenchanted when the friend proves to be only another self-absorbed, repetitious human after all.

Hazlitt's solution to the fraying of friendship is to force a break: "The only way to be reconciled with old friends is to part with them for good: at a distance we may chance to be thrown back (in a waking dream) upon old times and old feelings: or at any rate, we should not think of renewing our intimacy, till we have fairly *spit our spite*, or said, thought, and felt all the ill we can of each other." This is beautifully put (there's that Dostoevskian "spite" again), but I don't think it is such good advice; nor do I find Hazlitt to be the most trustworthy guide when it comes to maintaining extended relationships. At various points in this essay the reader may need to disengage from identifying with the author, while continuing to relish his energetic prose. (Nothing wrong with that: Hazlitt is a prickly loner and does not expect the reader to agree with everything he says—nor should any essayist worth his salt.) One of my favorite passages in any personal essay, for its comic daring, startling similes, and sheer cauterizing force, is this one that comes a few pages later, at the end of his remarks on friendship:

> The only intimacy I never found to flinch or fade was a purely intellectual one. There was none of the cant of candour in it, none of the whine of mawkish sensibility. Our mutual acquaintance were considered merely as objects of conversation and knowledge, not at all of affection. We regarded them no more in our experiments than 'mice in an air-pump:' or like malefactors, they were regularly cut down and given over to the dissecting knife. We spared neither friend nor foe. The skeleton of character might be seen, after the juice was extracted, dangling in the air like flies in cobwebs: or they were kept for future inspection in some refined acid. The demonstration was as beautiful as it was new. There is no surfeiting on gall: nothing keeps so well as a decoction of spleen. We grow tired of everything but turning others into ridicule, and congratulating ourselves on their defects.

Now, gossiping with a friend about the faults of other friends may not be the nicest behavior, but strictly speaking, it is not the same thing as hating. In fact, after its initial setup, the essay does not seem to be about hating at all, but rather about our inability to sustain enthusiasm. "We grow tired of everything." Hazlitt was above all an enthusiast, always on the lookout for the vital principle in art and life, who would ride his positive and negative excitements for as long as they could take him.

As though unaware that he has departed emotionally from the original promise of writing about hate, the logical side of Hazlitt continues to carry out his organizing scheme ("We hate old friends, we hate old books, we hate old opinions"): having examined friendship's durability, he then goes on to test his hypothesis by examining literature and the visual arts, two of the activities that have most sustained him: "We take a dislike to our favourite books, after a time, for the same reason. We cannot read the same works for ever. Our honeymoon, even though we wed the Muse, must come to an end; and is followed by indifference, if not by disgust. There are some works, those indeed that produce the most striking effect at first by novelty and boldness of outline, that will not bear reading twice: others of a less extravagant character, and that excite and repay attention by a greater nicety of details, have hardly interest enough to keep alive our continued enthusiasm." As for looking at favorite paintings (Hazlitt was an amateur painter): "The pleasure rises to its height in some moment of calm solitude or intoxicating sympathy, declines ever after, and from the comparison and a conscious falling-off, leaves rather a sense of satiety and irksomeness behind it . . . with all but those from Titian's hand." Again—at the risk of trying your patience—may I point out that what is being talked about here is indifference, satiety, at most disgust, and above all a failure to sustain enthusiasm. Not hatred. Not the *pleasures* of hating. The reason I harp on this point is that it took me so long to discover it: I had taught the essay at least twenty times before I perceived, at least on a conscious level, how much it had forsaken its original premise. Does that make the essay flawed? I don't think so. One of the great things about essays is that they can change direction, topic, and mood, as an essayist follows out his or her thoughts. Hazlitt probably needed the audacity of that title "On the Pleasure of Hating" to launch himself on an expedition around his discontents.

The last section is devoted to his political hopes. "As to my old opinions, I am heartily sick of them," he announces, and goes on a controlled rant about how disenchanted he has become. Hazlitt was part of that generation that regarded the dethroning of Louis XIV and the rise of democracies in America and France as the dawn of a new, better age. Napoleon, for all his dictatorial interest in power, was still seen by many progressives as spreading the values of liberty, equality, fraternity with his conquests, so that when he was defeated, and the forces of reaction restored the monarchy ("Legitimacy" was the term Hazlitt sneeringly invokes here), and when others, like Wordsworth, turned conservative with age, the essayist felt as though he alone had kept faith with his youthful ideals. He felt bitter and betrayed.

Betrayed not just politically but romantically. He had fallen in love with a barmaid, Sarah Walker, who seemed to lead him on, then reject him; the humiliating details of that sorry, failed courtship and erotic obsession were spelled out by Hazlitt himself in his courageous if scarily self-exposing account, *Liber Amoris*. Published anonymously in 1823, the book made him an object of ridicule and censure. It was this misadventure with Sarah that Hazlitt is undoubtedly referring to when he writes, "What chance is there of the success of real passion? What certainty of its continuance?"

He then goes into his summation, landing his final punch, as it were. If the essay has seemed to lose altitude in its transition from the crucial ruminations on friendship to the penultimate sections on reading, painting, and politics, the last two sentences restore it to a rhetorical height. Please notice how the first, the longer of these two sentences, keeps spiraling, eliminating yet another hope while sustaining syntactical suspense, before startling us with its conclusion. In this approach it recalls Keats's sonnet "When I Have Fears That I May Cease to Be," which darts from one syntactically unresolved anxiety to another for thirteen lines, until finally reaching its bleak release in the fourteenth line. Here is Hazlitt's closing:

> Seeing all this as I do, and unravelling the web of human life into its various threads of meanness, spite, cowardice, want of feeling, and want of understanding, of indifference towards others and ignorance of ourselves—seeing custom prevail over all excellence, itself giving way to infamy— mistaken as I have been in my public and private hopes, calculating others from myself, and calculating wrong: always disappointed where I placed most reliance: the dupe of friendship, and the fool of love; have I not reason to hate and despise myself? Indeed I do: and chiefly for not having hated and despised the world enough.

This misanthropic ending achieves many things at once. It connects back to the opening (the "web" reminding us of the spider); it pulls together all subsequent digressions as examples and, in labeling them like a medieval allegory about the seven deadly sins (meanness, spite, cowardice, custom, indifference, miscalculation, self-ignorance), argues for their place in a larger argument—argues, in effect, for the coherence of the essay itself—and returns us to the initial premise of the title by twice invoking the verb *to hate*. Good essays often hold off one final insight until the very end; the insight here is Hazlitt's self-hatred, which had not really been touched upon before, although he did foreshadow it with the phrase "at last we come to hate ourselves." Granted, he immediately shifts the hatred outward at the end, saying his problem was that he did not despise the world enough. But the genie has already been released: we are now conscious of the space that self-hatred occupied in all the preceding discontents.

This finale, wonderful as it is in summing up and joining together all the previous strands, nevertheless takes us to a gloomier, sourer place than is characteristic of the essay as a whole. Especially is this the case if you agree with my contention that the essay is more about the loss of friendship, the failure to sustain one's enthusiasms, and the inevitability of disillusionment than it is about the pleasure of hating. The ending takes sadistic (or is it masochistic?) glee in closing one door of hopeful consolation after another. It also leaves us with a caricature of Hazlitt as a low-grade paranoiac, a somewhat self-pitying victim who thinks himself betrayed by everyone. This isolation may make him more of an oddball, but to the detriment of his previous persona, that of an astute, compassionate observer offering solacing insight to everyone who is puzzled by the impermanence of love and friendship.

Those who have been taught to embrace love and kindness may refuse the bile at the essay's end, which says in effect that the world is rigged against happiness and the satisfactions of helping one another. Such readers doubtless love their spouses and their grandparents and probably do not agree with the author's whole enterprise. I respect their distaste for the piece. The tensions in Hazlitt—between the lover of humanity and the misanthrope, the warm enthusiast and the irritable cynic—are enacted without resolution or anything remotely soothing, and this makes some readers profoundly uncomfortable. I must admit I find these tensions stimulating and continue to be in thrall to Hazlitt's voice and his eloquent, take-no-prisoners sentences, which I believe capture a piece of disquieting truth about how threadbare our consolations may prove and how much we seem to need the thrill of rancor. "On the Pleasure of Hating" may not be a perfectly balanced essay, but it is, to my mind, a great one.

# How I Became an Emersonian

For several months I have been camping out in the mind of Ralph Waldo Emerson. It is a companionable, familiar, and yet endlessly stimulating place and, since his mind is stronger than mine, I keep deferring to his wisdom, even his doubts, and quite shamelessly identifying with him. All this started when I idly came across in a local bookstore the new, two-volume edition of his *Selected Journals*, published by the Library of America, and decided to give it a whirl. Some 1,800 pages later, I am in thrall to, in love with, Mr. Ralph Waldo Emerson. If this sounds homoerotic, so be it. I think of a peculiar passage about love in his journals that says that in embracing the worth of someone he admires, "I become his wife & he again aspires to a higher worth which dwells in another spirit & so is wife or receiver of that spirit's influence." In that respect, I have become Emerson's "wife," much to my surprise.

Truthfully, I never felt that close to Emerson in the past. I admired his prose style, but his essays seemed too impersonal for my taste. They sounded oracular, abstract, dizzyingly inspired, like visionary sermons: the thinking and language spectacular,

the man somehow missing. It took reading his journals to appreciate the man and the work.

The cliché rap on Emerson is that he was sententious, speaking through his nose "like a parson," in Melville's phrase; that he
was overly cheerful, a promoter of American exceptionalism and
individualism, therefore the friend of businessmen, not progressives. H. L. Mencken, who, along with his idol Nietzsche, had a
healthy respect for Emerson, wrote an essay about him called "An
Unheeded Law-Giver" that gets at some of the difficulty assessing
him: "Despite the vast mass of writing about him, he remains to be
worked out critically: practically all the existing criticism of him
is marked by his own mellifluous obscurity. Perhaps a good deal
of this obscurity is due to contradictions inherent in the man's
character. He was dualism ambulant." Mencken concluded that
his influence on our culture was nil: "There is, in the true sense,
no Emersonian school of American writers." Such an assessment
would have pleased Emerson, who wrote "This is my boast that
I have no school & no follower. I should account it a measure of
the impurity of thought, if it did not create independence." But if
Mencken is right that he lacks a school, I offer myself, if it's not
too late, as his pupil.

It would be foolhardy for me to pretend that Emerson has
been neglected. He has long been championed by some of our
leading critics, such as Richard Poirier, Harold Bloom, and Stanley Cavell; there is also a robust tradition of Emerson scholarship,
culminating in Robert D. Richardson's indispensable biography,
*Emerson: The Mind on Fire*, and his engaging sequel, *First We Read,
Then We Write*. Still, I sense a resistance to Emerson on the part
of the young, a falling out of fashion. Perhaps it is because he
was primarily an essayist, or perhaps Emerson has become an
afterthought in the American literary canon because he lacks that

outsider romance of our other mid-nineteenth-century giants. We tend to value renegades like Thoreau, doomed alcoholics like Poe, recluses like Dickinson, misunderstood visionaries like Melville, expansive gay bards like Whitman. Redskins, not palefaces (to use Philip Rahv's famous distinction).

Though Emerson began his journals as a dreamy would-be poet, he came to speak more and more in what Max Apple has called "the style of middle age." It is not as sexy as the style of youth, but it has its adherents, myself among them. According to Apple, "The style of middle age is a style of reappraisal, a style characterized by hesitation, by uncertainty, by the objects of the world rather than the passions that transport us from the world."

Ex-schoolmaster, ex-preacher, family man Emerson was quite aware of his problematic temperateness: "I hate scenes," he confided in his journal. "I think I have not the common degree of sympathy with dark, turbid, mournful, passionate natures. . . . In my strait & decorous way of living, native to my family & to my country, & more strictly proper to me, is nothing extravagant or flowing. I content myself with moderate languid actions, & never transgress the staidness of village manners. Herein I confess the poorness of my powers." Though phrased as an inadequacy, it is really stubbornness: he refuses to go to extremes. What needs to be understood is that, for Emerson, moderation was a tense, heroic agon.

He viewed many of his friends and colleagues as monomaniacs—zealots with a fixed idea. Attracted as he was to their ardor, critical of himself for a lack of "animal spirits," he also saw it as his particular mission to adhere to moderation. "Very hard it is to keep the middle point. It is a very narrow line," he wrote. And "Between narrow walls we walk—insanity on one side, and fat dullness on the other."

\* \* \*

In Emerson's journals you see how gradually, hesitantly, incrementally his belief system accrued over decades, through testing hunches and questioning himself. You also see the extent to which he took from other writers (his Big Ideas were syntheses, his throwaway perceptions truly original) and how much he was at the mercy of the disturbances of daily life. To oversimplify: the journals show his vulnerable side.

Unlike earlier abridgments of Emerson's journals, which had tended to reduce him to the Sage of Concord, this superlatively assembled Library of America selection, culled from the sixteen-volume Harvard complete edition by editor Lawrence Rosenwald, takes us right into the mind and heart of Emerson—bringing us closer perhaps than we come to any other American writer's thinking processes. And since Emerson was interested in practically everything, ancient and modern, we are treated to a remarkable range of thoughts, impulses, fears, enthusiasms, doubts, sorrows, analyses of friends, encounters with historical upheavals. Emerson began keeping the journals as an eighteen-year-old college student, and over the next fifty-seven years filled over 182 individual volumes. He never published them separately in his lifetime, but he consulted them extensively, taking months at a time to catalogue their contents, partly to make self-pillaging easier. Critics have often viewed the journals as merely a quarry for his essays and poems, but editor Rosenwald, who previously wrote *Emerson and the Art of the Diary*, argues that they were an intentional artwork—"his most successful experiment in creating a literary form."

Having sacrificed my summer to their 1,800 pages, I too am tempted to make enormous claims for them: that Emerson's journals are the lost ark of nineteenth-century American literature, the equivalent for literary nonfiction of *Moby Dick* in fiction or *Leaves of Grass* in poetry. The fact is that while they contain innumerable excitements, they also have plenty of dry patches; they are an archive of reflections, not a shaped work of art. Still, what I find inspirational about them is their faith in that old dream to which essayists, from Montaigne to the present, have been especially drawn: that you can start off writing about anything, however insignificant, and eventually all thoughts and digressions are somehow connected to each other by an invisible web.

At these journals' core is Emerson's sense that it is crucial to record one's fugitive ideas—to note "the meteorology of thought." He was indeed the weatherman of his own consciousness, charting his moods just as he observed on walks the changing aspects of nature and sky. What I respond to most in Emerson is his even-keeled preoccupation with daily life, the daily mental round, and with that, a resistance to the bullying aspects of apocalyptic dread. Not that the mind was always a comforting place to hang out: "There is something fearful in coming up against the walls of a mind & learning to describe their invisible circumference," he noted. Still, he valued weaving together "the threads that spin from a thought to a fact, & from one fact to another fact." Emerson's journals were this web, a grand attempt to test his intuition that a correspondence existed between nature's undulating patterns and the mind's ebb and flow.

Following in the footsteps of Plato and Montaigne, Emerson asserted that "the purpose of life seems to be to acquaint a man with himself," and he chose writing as the means to achieve self-knowledge. Since my literary patron saint is Montaigne as well, I was particularly gladdened to see how often Emerson professed in these journals his debt to the French author: "In Roxbury, in 1825, I read Cotton's translation of Montaigne. It seemed to me as if I had written the book myself in some former life, so sincerely it spoke to my thought & experience. No book before or since was ever so much to me as that." He kept going back to Montaigne, whom he found "full of fun, poetry, business, divinity, philosophy, anecdote, smut . . ." Though there's precious little smut in Emerson, he did take from Montaigne permission to enrich the staid Unitarianism of his upbringing with an earthier, more playful skepticism.

It is useful, up to a point, to think of Emerson as the American Montaigne. Both placed enormous faith in tracking their random thoughts and were, in effect, pioneering experimental scientists of consciousness, combing their mental lives for raw data; both believed that life was at bottom flux, transition, undulation; both openly borrowed from older writers yet insisted on cultivating idiosyncratic, outspoken honesty; both championed tolerance, moderation, and balance. Their differences were more temperamental than methodological: Montaigne arrived at an amused equanimity about his contradictions, while Emerson, descended from puritanical stock, worried his flaws and limitations more. Also, Emerson continued to hunger for a larger philosophical truth (his Transcendentalist notion of the Over-Soul) beneath the concrete material experiences that seemed sufficient for Montaigne. Stylistically, Montaigne's essays meander conversationally, whereas Emerson's are chiseled, taut. It is in his journals, more so than his essays, that Emerson reprises Montaigne's organic, improvisational approach.

Emerson's essays are dense with thought, requiring full attention every second; like a cliff face, they make purchase difficult. The notebooks are more appealingly relaxed. There is less pressure in them for every word to count. Emerson conveyed his aesthetic in advice to his wordy friend Bronson Alcott: "He should write that which cannot be omitted, every sentence a cube, standing on its bottom like a die, essential, immortal." Emerson's basic unit of composition *was* the sentence; he committed one amazing sentence after another. The result was an aphoristic compression in the essays that gives some readers the impression of entering a fog and not remembering after what exactly was said. I doubt that anyone who bothers to go through the journals can continue to dismiss Emerson as foggy. He is too clear and exposed in them.

Consider, for example, the opening of one of his best essays, "Circles":

> The eye is the first circle; the horizon which it forms is the second; and throughout nature this primary figure is repeated without end. It is the highest emblem in the cipher of the world. St. Augustine described the nature of God as a circle whose centre was everywhere, and the circumference nowhere. We are all our lifetime reading the copious sense of this first of forms. One moral we have already deduced, in considering the circular or compensatory character of every action. Another analogy we shall now trace; that every action admits to being outdone. Our life is an apprenticeship to the truth, that around every circle another can be drawn; that there is no end in nature, but every end is a beginning; that there is always another dawn risen on mid-noon, and under every deep a lower deep opens.

Dazzling stuff, if a bit abstract. In one paragraph you get impressions of the deity's shape, the law of compensation or karma, something like Nietzsche's eternal return, and of an alarming incompleteness. This news of the universe's dizzying uncertainty, circles under circles, is delivered in the confident, epigrammatic, impersonal "we" voice of Emerson the lawgiver: like a set of mathematical formulas with intransitive verbs as equation signs. It would be hard to predict where such an essay is headed from this opening. A philosophical meditation on circularity? Possibly, though often any attempt to negotiate Emerson's essays reminds me of his journal comment, "I found when I had finished my new lecture that it was a very good house, only the architect had unfortunately omitted the stairs." In that one sentence we hear the humor, self-deprecating awareness, and personal voice of the journals.

His addresses and essays (both delivered orally, since he made his living largely as a public speaker) show Emerson trying to win over an audience with persuasive rhetoric. Not so the journals, which he wrote for himself alone and could therefore be more cantankerous or frank in them. Take the direct aggression of this journal passage: "Another vice of manners which I do not easily forgive is the dullness of perception which talks to every man alike. As soon as I perceive that my man does not know me, but is making his speech to the man that happens to be here, I wish to gag him." One thing Emerson did not like about many reformers, he says in these journals, is that they speak to everyone alike. They lack interiority, and for Emerson, conversation was ideally a space where interiorities could be exchanged. But he had mixed feelings about how much he *could* rely on other people, or they on him, and always wondered if he would be better off alone. This conflict between the gregarious and the solitary pulls of his nature never ceased to perplex him. I understand the dilemma.

Happily domesticated one moment, fiercely resistant to family life the next: I confess that here I most identify with him. My wife says to me, "In your head you're still a bachelor." I am tempted to counter with Elizabeth Hardwick's statement, "All writing is profoundly unmarried." Is living in one's head the special malady of writers, or is it the universal human condition? Like most married people, Emerson expressed ambivalence about "the vitriolic acid of marriage," wondering if writers ought even to be married, while elsewhere saying that "Marriage is the perfection that love aimed at, ignorant of what it sought." If you read between the journals' lines, it would appear the Emersons had a decent if forbearing marriage.

Sometimes Emerson reminds me of Tolstoy's Pierre at the end of *War and Peace*, wandering off from the nursery and the dinner party to gaze inquisitively at the stars. Intimacy demands make him uneasy, worried as he is that he might not be able to meet them, either because he was protecting his inner life and writing space, or because, as he feared, he lacked the necessary warmth. Invariably courteous to neighbors and importuning strangers—"Politeness was invented by wise men to keep fools at a distance," he wrote—it pained him when his New England reserve kept him from honoring a loved one's or friend's neediness. One such crisis occurred when Margaret Fuller, the feminist and Transcendentalist, taxed him "with inhospitality of soul," for keeping her at a distance with "literary gossip"—for holding back. "I thought of my experience with several persons which resembled this: and confessed that I would not converse with the divinest person more than one week." How refreshing that is! In a later entry, he puzzled over "these strange, cold-warm, attractive-repelling conversations with Margaret, whom I always admire, most revere when I nearest see, and sometimes love, yet whom I freeze, and who freezes me to silence, when we seem to promise to come nearest." In the end Emerson and Fuller did work out a satisfying friendship, and when she drowned, in that ghastly accident off Fire Island, he wrote a generous memoir of her (though privately recording in his journals that her genius resided in conversation, not in writing).

Readers today may wonder if Fuller had sexual designs on Emerson. That was probably not the case. Rather, when the members of the Transcendentalist circle, each grown up as brilliant isolates in mercantile America, found one another, living in the same Boston-Concord area, it must have awakened such hunger for soul communion as could never be properly slaked. Beyond that, everyone around Emerson seemed to seek his approval: he had become a benign father figure from his late thirties. Compounding the problem was Emerson's acute loneliness and his paradoxical need for solitude. Only in solitude could he attempt to free himself from public opinion and discern his own mind. "Alone is wisdom. Alone is happiness. Society nowadays makes us lowspirited, hopeless. Alone is heaven." At the same time he felt the failure of most attempts at empathy: "Man is insular, and cannot be touched. Every man is an infinitely repellent orb." This melancholy conviction of universal solipsism was the reverse side of Emerson's advocacy of self-reliance.

When Hawthorne died, Emerson regretted that they had never become friends: "It would have been a happiness, doubtless to both of us, to have come into habits of unreserved intercourse. It was easy to talk with him,—there were no barriers,—only, he said so little, that I talked too much. . . . Now it appears that I waited too long."

Talking too little was not Henry David Thoreau's problem. He and Emerson sustained a close friendship for decades. This is in spite of the fact that Thoreau was, according to his friend, almost incessantly combative and self-absorbed. "It is curious that Thoreau goes to a house to say with little preface what he has just read or observed, delivers it in a lump, is quite inattentive to comment or thought which any of the company offer on the matter, is merely interrupted by it, & when he has finished his report, departs with precipitation." Emerson oscillated between being enchanted and annoyed by his friend's eccentricities. Privately he worried that Thoreau's going to jail was "one step to suicide" and that his retreat to the woods might end in "want & madness." ("My dear Henry," he wrote in his journals, "a frog was made to live in a swamp, but a man was not made to live in a swamp.") But it was he who urged Thoreau to keep a journal, and he copied pages of Thoreau's entries into his own notebook, paying him the compliment that Thoreau's "flesh and blood" writing went "a step beyond" anything he was capable of doing. True enough, Thoreau managed to get more gristle and loam into his prose than Emerson, who was always tilting his sentences toward abstraction. Thoreau was the quintessential bachelor; Emerson the householder and family man who took him into his home when the woodsman got tired of camping outdoors. Though they did quarrel for a time, as was inevitable, they reconciled with a conversation about "the Eternal loneliness" of everyone they knew, including themselves.

What impresses me the most about Emerson is that, keenly aware of his own limitations, he still tried to stretch himself to accommodate others and to become larger-souled, more responsive. "Better be a nettle in the side of your companion than be his echo," he wrote, and some of his friends were indeed nettles. He put up with the quirks of friends like the mad poet Jones Very; he invited Thoreau and Fuller to live with his family; he even forced himself to abandon his cherished spectator role and become a political activist.

The transition to political activist took a while. He felt his task in life was to write, not agitate: "My way to help the government is to write sonnets." He sent an open letter to President Martin Van Buren deploring the government's ill-treatment of the Cherokees but disliked doing it. Privately he recorded in journals his liberal views on every issue of the day: he was for abolition of slavery, for women's suffrage and property rights, against the removal of the American Indians from their land, for the new immigrants, against the cannibalistic aspects of capitalism and the selfishness of the wealthy class, and unequivocally against U.S. imperialism. Stating that "Nationalism is babyishness for the most part," he opposed the Mexican War, Texas's annexation, the expropriation of Hawaii. But still, he insisted on clinging to "inaction, this wise passiveness, until my hour comes when I can see how to act with truth."

His hour finally arrived around 1851, when he became outraged at the Fugitive Slave Act, which stated that runaway slaves must be returned to their owners in the South. He filled dozens of pages with fulmination against the traitorous statesman Daniel Webster, who voted for the bill to placate the South; he was horrified that "this filthy enactment was made in the 19th Century, by people who could read & write. I will not obey it, by God." Emerson now began speaking out widely for abolition, even getting booed on occasion.

His ardent defense of blacks may seem a change of heart, after some condescending remarks he had made about "the Negro race" years earlier. But that was Emerson's way: not to deny himself entering any stray thought in the journals, however lopsided, and then to come around to the most reasonable position. Just as he made it a point to listen to both sides of every question, so he attended to the split voices in his own thinking. A walking dualism, as Mencken said, Emerson, always on the lookout for wisdom, was never complacent. "Wisdom consists in keeping the soul liquid, or, in resisting the tendency to too rapid putrefaction," he wrote.

One of the ways Emerson staved off illiquidity was by reading. Having consumed the English classics, he taught himself German, French, and Italian, translated Dante's *La Vita Nuova*, and immersed himself in the Bhagavad Gita, the Koran, Buddhist texts, and Persian poets. He wished he could satisfy his curiosity about Egyptian history, Sanskrit literature, and the Chaldaic oracles. He admired his idol Goethe as much for the German polymath's study of optics and plants as for writing *Faust*. That nineteenth-century bug of believing one could synthesize all knowledge and spirit had bitten Emerson. In Eastern thought he found, at times, a model for that integration.

Given that he was cleverer and better read than most of his countrymen, his modesty came as a surprise to me. His journals frequently expressed admiration of farmers, workmen, voluble Italians. "My only secret was that all men were my masters. I never saw one who was not my superior." I take heart from Emerson's inferiority complex. For a long while he longed for a spiritual guide, a superior being who could lead him upward. But he concluded in the end that one must seek the God within.

Emerson's doctrine of self-reliance, which has been misunderstood and oversimplified, did not deny that man was a social animal. On a daily level, he practiced building community and fulfilling civic and neighborly responsibilities; he edited magazines, got friends' books published, attended local meetings. But he advocated that Americans should stop taking all their cultural cues from Europe, and those seeking spiritual truth should put aside "a historical Christianity . . . Christ preaches the greatness of Man but we hear only the greatness of Christ." In a sense it was easier for a man like Emerson, already so steeped in European culture and Christian tradition, to argue for going one's own way. He was convinced that every person contained within a vision of the Perfect, an enormous sun-like potential that could only be realized by breaking away from conventional thought. "We are all very near to sublimity. . . . Whilst we are waiting we beguile the time, one with jokes, one with sleep, one with eating, one with crimes." Just as we waste our inner sublime, so the outer world brings us a daily abundance, which we seem ill-equipped to harvest. In an especially lovely sentence he wrote, "The days come & go like muffled & vague figures sent from a distant friendly party, but they say nothing, & if we do not use the gifts they bring, they carry them as silently away." I must say that, being more pragmatic, I do not share this vision of man's unrealized divinity. But I am with him all the way when he expresses dissatisfaction with life, sounding like one of Chekhov's characters: "I find no good lives. I would live well. I seem to be free to do so, yet I think with very little respect of my way of living; it is weak, partial, not full & not progressive. But I do not see any other that suits me better." He put it even more succinctly: "We are all dying of miscellany."

Among Emerson's most attractive qualities, to my mind, was that he never overdramatized himself or exaggerated the nobility of his sentiments. He took careful note when indifference or coldness had crept into his soul, and as a result, his sympathies sound more trustworthy. Though he believed human beings are made for ecstasy and chastised himself for not feeling enough joy, a work-centered Stoicism remained his default mode. This was not so much resignation as resilience, predicated on the understanding that human beings can take a lot. The one thing he resisted was embracing suffering in order to feel deeper. "We court suffering in the hope that here at least we shall find reality, sharp angular peaks and edges of truth. But it is scene painting, a counterfeit, a goblin." His secret (a goal disdained by youth but not middle age) was to have achieved a gyroscopic equilibrium. He confessed, "I told J.V. [the poet Jones Very] that I had never suffered, & that I could scarce bring myself to feel a concern for the safety & life of my nearest friends that would satisfy them: that I saw clearly that if my wife, my child, my mother, should be taken from me, I should remain whole with the same capacity of cheap enjoyment from all things." This alarmingly candid, disturbing statement seems an admission of shallowness, or at least the lack of a tragic consciousness.

But he spoke too soon; he would shortly come to know suffering. If it had eluded him after the death of his first wife, Ellen, whom he incorporated into an angelic myth (his second wife even collaborated in this maudlin altar worship by suggesting they name their daughter Ellen), he had no such protection when he lost his firstborn, Waldo. Emerson had delighted in recording the sayings and deeds of this charming son, and when the boy died of a sudden illness at age eight, he felt only devastation: "The wonderful Boy is gone . . . he most beautiful of children is not here. I comprehend nothing of this fact but its bitterness." In the passages grieving Waldo we get the rock-bottom Emerson, without disguises. He recovered his equanimity but never his optimism after Waldo's death. Decades later, he would recall Waldo at the circus watching the clown's antics and saying, " 'It makes me want to go home,' and I am forced to quote my boy's speech often and often since. I can do so few things, I can see so few companies, that do not remind me of it." The distance between public and private man was never more starkly put. Those who regard Emerson as too cheerful would do well to ponder his statement, "After thirty a man wakes up sad every morning."

The journals frequently help us to grasp the confessional nature of the essays. For instance, in his essay "Experience" there is this dazzling sentence, offered without elaboration: "The only thing grief has taught me, is to know how shallow it is." The journals contain numerous passages about working through grief, such as this one: "Presently the man is consoled, but not by the fine things; no, but perhaps by the very foul things, namely, by the defects of the dead from which he shall no more suffer; or, what often happens, by being relieved from relations & responsibility, to which he was unequal." This last bit, about suspecting oneself unequal to the challenge of caring for the infirm, is typical of Emerson's compulsive honesty, no matter under how bad a light it might place him. The journal's entry is not as spectacular as the essay sentence, but it gives us a more shaded insight into the psychology of grief.

In his review of the journals in *The New York Review of Books*, Robert Pogue Harrison raises an interesting point: "One difference between Emerson's journals and his essays is that the former contain a much fuller record of both worlds [his speculations and empirical evidence drawn from city and farm], in their uneasy interaction, while the essays for the most part reflect only the world of Emerson's thought. Those of us who are more taken by Emerson's thinking than by his life prefer his essays to his journals for precisely that reason." I would only qualify this judgment by saying the choice is a somewhat false one, since the journals give us in full Emerson's thinking *about* his life. Harrison goes on to write, "What is missing in the essays, by contrast, is a record of the heroic efforts it cost Emerson to maintain the unconditional trust he had in himself, and to avoid its opposite, which is despair." In that respect, yes, I do seem to be siding with those who are more taken by his life: through the journals, Emerson has become a model for me of how to overcome anxiety and despair and stay on an even keel.

Trying to juggle all his social ties in middle age, he threatened wryly to close up shop. "A man of 45 does not want to open new accounts of friendship. He has said Kitty kitty long enough." Nevertheless, he remained receptive to new acquaintance, helping younger people get started. The episode with Walt Whitman is legendary. Emerson wrote Whitman not only his famous endorsement but several letters of recommendation to secure Whitman a post in Washington. They met a number of times. Whitman recalled years later, "I think everyone was fascinated by his personality. His usual manner carried with it something penetrating and sweet beyond mere description. There is in some men an indefinable something which flows out and over you like a flood of light—as if they possessed it illimitably—their whole being suffused with it. Being—in fact that is precisely the word. Emerson's whole attitude shed forth such an impression. . . . Never a face more gifted with power to express, fascinate, maintain."

We can stare at his photographs and guess at the power "the gentle Emerson" had for his contemporaries. Or we can turn to the writing, especially the journals, where his wholeness of being is manifest. In later years he was introduced to President Lincoln, and celebrated as the nation's foremost public intellectual. Self-mockingly, he said if the people who were honoring his intellect had read the same books he had, they wouldn't think he was so smart.

Facing the indignities of aging, he had a mixed response. On the plus side, he no longer felt the need to prove himself: "It is long already fixed what I can & what I cannot do." On the minus side, he wrote, "'Tis strange, that it is not in vogue to commit hari-kari as the Japanese do at 60. Nature is *so* insulting in her hints & notices, does not pull you out by the sleeve, but pulls out your teeth, tears off your hair in patches, steals your eyesight, twists your face into an ugly mask, in short, puts all contumelies upon you, without in the least abating your zeal to make a good appearance, and all this at the same time that she is moulding the new figures around you into wonderful beauty which, of course, is almost making your plight worse."

I'm sure the case could be made for Emerson's relevance by casting him as a proto-postmodernist, a wild man with dark imagination, or a proponent of multicultural diversity. My fondness for him rests on his intelligence and his truthfulness, his questing, nondogmatic sanity. He wrote some of the best reflective prose we have; he was a hero of intellectual labor, a loyal friend, and, taking all flaws into account, a good egg. True, he was a bourgeois and wrote in the style of middle age. Can we ever forgive him? I can. More, I can identify with him, having at last entered both categories. In middle age, I find myself an unrepentent Emersonian. I simply like the man, which is saying something after having spent 1,800 pages in the innermost chamber of his mind. Of how many other American writers could one say the same?

# Teaching James Baldwin

Whenever I have taught the literature of personal essays, with an eye to motivating students to write their own, I have relied on James Baldwin's work, knowing that he will engage high school and college kids with excitement. The resistance they show to Lamb, Hazlitt, Montaigne, and all those other "old-time writers" seems to melt away under Baldwin's fiery gaze. It is Jimmy to the rescue, in part because his honesty and passion are very attractive to young people, but also because Baldwin dramatized adolescence again and again as his own particular crucible of selfhood—boy preacher, loss of faith, yearnings to write, father's death, the forgoing of college, struggles over racial bitterness and sexual preference—and sympathized so warmly with the efforts of all youth to forge an identity.

In an essay entitled "They Can't Turn Back," on the students trying to desegregate southern schools, he writes, parenthetically and characteristically, about the

> really agonizing privacy of the very young. They are only beginning to realize that the world is difficult and dangerous, that they are, themselves, tormentingly complex

---

and that the years that stretch before them promise to be more dangerous than the years that are behind. And they always seem to be wrestling, in a private chamber to which no grownup has access, with monumental decisions. Everyone laughs at himself once he has come through this storm, but it is borne in on me, suddenly, that it *is* a storm, a storm, moreover, that not everyone survives and through which no one comes unscathed. Decisions made at this time always seem and, in fact, nearly always turn out to be decisions that determine the course and quality of a life. I wonder for the first time what it can be like to be making, in the adolescent dark, such decisions as this generation of students has made.

This is catnip to the young.

I am being ironic because, while I love Baldwin's essayistic manner, I sometimes feel that I have to exert counterpressure to pry students from its appeal and to exercise a little skeptical critical intelligence. Once they fall under the spell of his voice, they tend to buy into his whole analysis of race, politics, America—the bombastically wrongheaded prophetic parts as well as the sensible ones. What they really buy into is his presentation of self as a wounded human being: there can be no doubt that, in our talk show culture, which enshrines victimhood, Baldwin plays exceedingly well.

When I teach Baldwin I focus on his essays, because I think he is a great essayist—indeed, the most important American essayist since the end of World War II—and only a so-so fiction writer. His long novels, *Another Country* and *Just Above My Head*, now seem windy and unfocused; *Giovanni's Room*, stronger but somewhat precious. If there is enough time, I have occasionally assigned *Go Tell It on the Mountain*, which many consider his best novel, just to show how the same autobiographical material (a Harlem adolescence) may be treated in fiction and nonfiction. To my mind this first novel of Baldwin's, atmospheric as it is, cannot hold a candle to his infinitely more expressive personal essay, "Notes of a Native Son."

A twenty-page miracle, a masterpiece of compression, "Notes of a Native Son" seems to pour out in a white heat of emotional prose, though it is everywhere artfully shaped. The portrait of his father, David Baldwin (whom he later learned was actually his stepfather, though he never went back and altered the essay to reflect that fact), is a model of unsentimental ambivalence. Many students, encountering it for the first time, are shocked to see that one can actually tell such tales out of school. Baldwin's ferocious and fastidious candor liberates them to begin considering the meanings of their own parents' lives in their writing.

A good place to focus is this amazing paragraph:

He was, I think, very handsome. I gather this from photographs and from my own memories of him, dressed in his Sunday best and on his way to preach a sermon somewhere, when I was little. Handsome, proud, and ingrown, "like a toenail," somebody said. But he looked to me, as I grew older, like pictures I had seen of African tribal chieftains: he really should have been naked, with warpaint on and barbaric mementos, standing among spears. He could be chilling in the pulpit and indescribably cruel in his personal life and he was certainly the most bitter man I have ever met; yet it must be said that there was something else in him, buried in him, which lent him his tremendous power and, even, a rather crushing charm. It had something to do with his blackness, I think—he was very black—with his blackness and his beauty, and with the fact that he knew he was black but did not know that he was beautiful. He claimed to be proud of his blackness but it had also been the cause of much humiliation and it had fixed bleak boundaries to his life. He was not a young man when we were growing up and he had already suffered many kinds of ruin; in his outrageously demanding and protective way he loved his children, who were black and menaced, like him; and all these things sometimes showed in his face when he tried, never to my knowledge with any success, to establish contact with any of us. When he took one of his children on his knee to play, the child always became fretful and began to cry; when he tried to help one of us with our homework the absolutely unabating tension which emanated from him caused our minds and our tongues to become paralyzed, so that he, scarcely knowing why, flew into a rage and the child, not knowing why, was punished. If it ever entered his head to bring a surprise home for his children, it was, almost unfailingly, the wrong surprise and even the big watermelons he often brought home on his back in the summertime led to the most appalling scenes. I do not remember, in all those years, that one of his children was ever glad to see him come home. From what I was able to gather of his early life, it seemed that this inability to establish contact with other people had always marked him and had been one of the things which had driven him out of New Orleans. There was something in him, therefore, groping and tentative, which was never expressed and which was buried with him. One saw it most clearly when he was facing new people and hoping to impress them. But he never did, not for long. We went from church to smaller and more improbable church, he found himself in less and less demand as a minister, and by the time he died none of his friends had come to see him for a long time. He had lived and died in an intolerable bitterness of spirit and it frightened me, as we drove him to the graveyard through these unquiet, ruined streets, to see how powerful and overflowing this bitterness could be and to realize that this bitterness now was mine.

It's all there, in this paragraph, but it requires some unpacking: Baldwin's sheer love of language; his intoxication with adjectives and adverbs, at a time when other writers were starting to avoid them; his King James Bible rhythms, oral sermon repetitions, and anaphoric series ("and/and" "blackness/blackness"); his oxymorons ("crushing charm"); his witheringly undercutting use of interpolated phrases ("never to my knowledge with any success"); his anglicisms ("rather" or the impersonal pronoun "one"); his verbal arrows, conjunctions, and pointers ("yet it must be said" "therefore"); his ability to sustain an extremely long sentence without wearying or confusing his reader, then employ short sentences or sentence fragments for variety; his willingness to pull back from a specific detail and make the broader generalization; his balance between rejection and tenderness, between angry truths and forgiveness; his ennoblings ("tribal chieftains") and deflations, often in the same sentence; his detachment and grim humor; and finally, his generous move to identify with, show complicity with, the flaw ("this bitterness") he had seemed to be indicting.

Baldwin's prose is a carefully crafted, self-conscious, mannered (in the best sense) performance, and part of what I do when I teach him is to draw attention to his techniques. Students tend to inhale powerful prose in an undifferentiated rush, and I want to slow them down. Of course I don't wish to dilute with English teacher pedantry their feeling for this person who has suffered and witnessed great suffering, but I want them to understand the victory over language that Baldwin accomplished, because this is part of the positive side of the ledger that helped him survive— and may help them survive.

I try to get them to write a portrait of their father or mother, and to reflect on how we assimilate the traits of our parents, for better or for worse. Or I ask them to write about some incident in which anger got the better of them, or to consider in an essay the nature of bitterness. Or just write about their growing up. By the time they have finished reading "Notes from a Native Son," they have often gotten the point—the challenge to be as honest and personally revealing as possible on the page—and don't need much specific prodding to be off and running.

I follow it with as many Baldwin essays as I can, because I find that he is one of those writers whom students are willing to be saturated by. The more they read him, the more comfortable they become with his strategic moves and ranges of interest, and the more he seems a friend. Ideally, I can assign as a text the *Collected Essays* published by the Library of America, though one can get by in a pinch with the earlier paperback editions, such as *Notes of a Native Son*, *Nobody Knows My Name*, and *The Fire Next Time*, which are still in print. I ask them to read such gems as "Equal in Paris," a narrative vignette about getting arrested, "Stranger in the Village," a meditation on otherness and the expatriate experience, "The Harlem Ghetto," just to show how fully formed a stylist he was at twenty, "Alas, Poor Richard," a searching double portrait of Baldwin and his fatherly mentor/rival Richard Wright, "Sweet Lorraine," about the playwright Lorraine Hansberry, and, of course, *The Fire Next Time*.

This double essay has autobiographical passages as great as anything Baldwin ever wrote. You may have to supply some historical context for students (the mood of the sixties, the civil rights movement, the Black Muslims, Malcolm X, etc.), though I have found that on the whole they get it. A bigger problem is the one I alluded to earlier: when this ambitious mélange of an essay begins to fall apart, the smoothness of Baldwin's writing may fool students into not even questioning his rhetorical overkill. *The Fire Next Time*, for all its magnificent writing, gets entangled in its own rhetoric toward the end, as Baldwin invokes preacher-fashion the image of cosmic apocalypse. Essentially he is saying that if America doesn't support revolutions at home and abroad, it will be burned to the ground. This is always a risky maneuver when addressing an American society that keeps managing, rightly or wrongly, not to go up in smoke.

Baldwin may have been carried away to this apocalyptic position not only by the momentary logic of historic crisis but by the frustration of having to bring a long, increasingly complex essay to robust conclusion. His later, book-length essays, *No Name in the Street* and *The Devil Finds Work* and *The Evidence of Things Not Seen*, end with similar, unsatisfactory warnings of "the wrath to come" or bromides to love one another. The more Baldwin was drawn to longer discursive meditations, an impulse admirably Montaigne-like, the more he dared to enter the oceanic swell of the extended essay. But the difficulty was that he was trying to report the social problems of an America he had become distant from while living abroad, and so he kept going off on digressive riffs and not being able to get out of them, and gave in to the impulse to finish with a sermon about heaven and hell, which he knew he would know how to deliver.

His later full-length essays are fascinating to teach, partly because they have such wonderful patches and partly because they don't really hold together. It's salutary, I think, for students to realize that the structural problems of extended essays may be so daunting that even a master of the form can get bogged down.

In certain ways the extra-long essay *was* a compatible form for Baldwin, in that it brought out relaxed, self-surprising passages such as nothing else could. But he never figured out how to pull it off artistically, how to tie up the loose ends or give it an inevitable shape. (Not that so many equally brilliant modern essayists have, either: consider, for instance, Virginia Woolf's struggles to batten down *A Room of One's Own* or *Three Guineas*.)

There are lessons anyone attempting to write personal essays can learn from Baldwin. How to dramatize oneself, for instance. Many personal essays misfire because of the blandness of the narrative persona, but this was never a problem for James Baldwin: he could always project himself on paper as in the midst of some burning conflict or dire strait. He was a bit of an actor, which an essayist needs to be—willing and able to adopt different masks.

Another of his admirable qualities was a self-reflective insight that let the reader follow his thinking process. Six pages into "Alas, Poor Richard," we encounter this stopped-in-our-tracks passage:

> I was far from imagining, when I agreed to write this memoir, that it should prove to be such a painful and difficult task. What, after all, can I really say about Richard . . . ? Everything founders in the sea of what might have been. We might have been friends, for example, but I cannot honestly say that we were. There might have been some way of avoiding our quarrel, our rupture; I can only say that I failed to find it. The quarrel having occurred, perhaps there might have been a way to have become reconciled. I think, in fact, that I counted on this coming about in some mysterious, irrevocable way, the way a child dreams of winning, by means of some dazzling exploit, the love of his parents.

I began by implying that James Baldwin had in some way fixated on his adolescent crisis and thereby overstated the part of the victim. But we see from this passage how wrong, or incomplete, my assessment was; for this passage demonstrates the worldly, sorrowful realism and willingness to take responsibility for one's fate that made Baldwin, at his best, a hero of American maturity. Perhaps what finally explains his attractiveness to young people is the way he epitomizes the process of becoming a thoughtful, stoical adult, without losing touch with the still-youthful part of him that had been so exposed and nearly defenseless in growing up.

# Edward Hoagland: The Dean
## of American Essayists

There is probably no essayist today who has earned more respect from his peers and fellow practitioners than Edward Hoagland. John Updike called him "the best essayist of my generation," Philip Roth said he was "America's most intelligent and wide-ranging essayist-naturalist," and Joyce Carol Oates described him evocatively as "our Chopin of the genre." He has also been a crucial model for younger environmental writers, such as Gretel Ehrlich, Bill McKibben, and Scott Russell Sanders.

A novelist or poet of his accomplishments would be receiving lengthy career assessments and White House invitations at this point in his career, whereas Hoagland's books are now consigned to small presses and a smattering of reviews. While this neglect may be merely another sign of the public's larger indifference to literature, it could also have something to do with the author himself. For Hoagland is a most peculiar writer, an intricate stylist whose prose seems rooted in a venerable tradition that resists speed-reading, and who has obstinately staked out two territories, the ruminative (as opposed to the narrative) personal essay and nature writing, which are among the least commercially catching. Regardless, his skill at composing sentences remains undimmed. There is something very moving about a master personal essayist continuing to articulate the challenges of life right up to the end, no matter what size the readership.

Since Hoagland draws unreservedly on autobiographical elements, even his most casual readers will be familiar with that life's leitmotifs. He was born in 1932 in New York City; when he was eight his family moved to rural Connecticut and he discovered the joys of roaming outdoors. His father, a straitlaced, bigoted Republican lawyer who canceled his subscription to the Metropolitan Opera after the black contralto Marian Anderson sang there, and would later disinherit his two children when they got divorced, provided an ideal target for rebellion.

Partly under the stress of this disapproving parent, Hoagland developed a serious stutter, which would influence his loner personality and career choices: "A stutter pushes you to the margins anyhow. How will you land a teaching job, a chance in journalism, or simply chat up an intriguing person at a party?" He went to Harvard and worked summers in the circus, where he tended the lions, tigers, and other beasts. The circus would provide the milieu for his first novel, *Cat Man* (1955), published when he was only twenty-two. He served in the army, worked briefly in a morgue, and in short acquired the kind of résumé that used to appear on the bios of novelists before there were MFA programs.

Hoagland had dreamed of being a fiction writer, but after publishing three early novels, "in my thirties I realized my aptitudes were better suited to essay writing." He's at his best not when telling a conventional story but when he circles a subject from many vantage points, teasing and digressing, piling up gorgeously angled syntaxes and frank admissions while frustrating tidy conclusions—all hallmarks of a true essayist.

He began to have success placing essays in magazines such as *The Atlantic*, *The New Yorker*, and *Sports Illustrated*. One of Hoagland's fortes is his description of animals, which led to his classic pieces on turtles, black bears, cows, and red wolves. He commented wryly on his affinity for animals and his urge to defend endangered species in a passage from the beautiful 1974 essay "Lament the Red Wolf":

> The most vivid observation to be made about animal enthusiasts—both the professionals who work in the field and, in particular, the amateurs—is that they are split between the rosiest, well-adjusted sort of souls and the wounded and lame. (More professionals are rosy, more amateurs are lame.) Animals used to provide a lowlife way to kill and get away with it, as they do still, but, more intriguingly, for some people they are an aperture through which wounds drain. The scapegoat of olden times, driven off for the bystanders' sins, has become a tender thing, a running injury. There, running away—save it, save it—is me: hurt it and you are hurting me.*

He went periodically on the road and excelled at travel writing, specializing in British Columbia and Africa. Women captivated him: having discovered that they were more than tolerant of his stutter, seeing it as a charming vulnerability, he consequently stuttered less around them. Eventually he learned to control the speech defect enough to teach writing and literature in a half-dozen universities. In the meantime he went through two marriages and many affairs. His second marriage, to Marion

---

* See *Heart's Desire: The Best of Edward Hoagland*, Summit Books, 1988—a collection of greatest hits, and probably still the best place to start reading this author.

Magid, an editor at *Commentary*, produced his daughter, Molly, and lasted for twenty-five years.

In the 1980s he felt impelled to move out of the city to be closer to nature: he now divides his time between Martha's Vineyard and Vermont, where he lives a third of the year alone in the woods without electricity. During his sixties he went partially blind, depressing him to the point of contemplating suicide; fortunately, he found a surgeon who was able to restore his sight. Hoagland continues to publish contemplative essays in places like *Harper's* and *The American Scholar*.

An assortment of pieces from recent years forms his new essay collection (his tenth), *Sex and the River Styx*, a book held together by persistent burrowing around in the themes of old age, dying, ecstasy, balance, and the fate of the planet. Hoagland, approaching eighty, has been moved to take stock of his past behavior, to ready himself for the end of life, and to contemplate what sort of world will outlive him. Overall, he finds no major regrets: searching his conscience, he locates "no indelibly shameful acts." He has seen enough places. He does not fear death, he says, especially given the coming storm: "Death will save me from witnessing the drowned polar bears, smashed elephant herds, wilting frog populations, squashed primate refuges." Being a firm believer in the nitrogen cycle, Hoagland welcomes the chance for the worms to have at him, to recycle him. But if that is the long view, he wonders, then why does he still brood about past mistakes, lapsed friendships, failed marriages, ex-lovers? If he's going to become a bug, "why, then, care so much about the moral timbre of the life I've led?" A good question. To his credit, he is still struggling to figure it out.

The opening essay, "Small Silences," is a superb demonstration of Hoagland at his most appealing and unfettered. He begins with lyrical recollections of his childhood move to Connecticut during World War II, and the discovery of the pond. " 'I'm going to the pond,' I'd say casually to my mother; then dodge carefully past" the neighbor's servant

> toward the trillium and columbine, the toadstools and fairy-ring mushrooms, the nematodes and myriapods, the blueberries or blackberries, near the opaque yet shiny stretch of hidden water, deep here, shallow there, with the wind ruffling the surface to conceal such factual matters, and cold at its inlet but warm where it fed into a creek that ran to the Silvermine River and finally the ocean.

This characteristic sentence takes the reader into a forest of sensory description, replete with names of flora and fauna, listed for the sheer joy of it, and then scoots off in a surprising conclusion.

> I'd lie on my back on a patch of moss watching a swaying poplar's branches interlace with another's, and the tremulous leaves vibrate, and the clouds forgather to parade zoologically overhead, and felt linked to the whole matrix, as you either do or you don't through the rest of your life.

The key word here is "linked": the author sees himself as a later-day American Transcendentalist, sensing a rapturous immanent connection among all living things. Nature, he says, "speaks in terms of glee. Glee is like the froth on beer or cocoa." He keeps wondering about joy's evolutionary function: "But what explains the elation, exuberance—the surplus snap of well-being that animals as well as naturalists feel?" This insistence on ebullience as the thread that holds together Creation is essential as an optimistic counterweight to the gloomy bad news about nature's potential demise.

The defect of much environmental writing in our time is its self-righteousness and solemnity, its general shortage of humor, irony, wit. Regardless of how dire the situation may be and how correct are those sounding the alarm, their warnings do not often make for stimulating prose. Hoagland does not want to be a scold—or only a scold. Lamenting the extinction of so many species in one generation, he recognizes that not everyone sees this or cares: "But the survival of wild places and wild things, like the permanence of noteworthy architecture, or the opera, or a multiplicity of languages, or old shade trees in old neighborhoods, is not a priority for most people."

His own method of observation is very precise: "Nature is nuance, like fireflies and foxfire light, not bullet-train scenery. Half a dozen cedar waxwings perched side by side on a branch will pass a wild cherry back and forth along the row before one of them finally, decorously eats it." He worries less about his personal death than the passing of nature hobbyists as a group. When he and his kind are gone, "who is going to notice all this stuff? And yet if people don't, it will vanish faster." Elsewhere in the book he writes, "I'm ready for somebody else to take a turn at doing the observing and let me join that black-and-yellow salamander under the log to wait out the emergencies." But the disappearance of nature lore as common knowledge is disturbing: "To lose moonlight, and compass placement, and grasshoppers telling us the temperature by the intensity of their sound, poses the question of whether we can safely do away with everything else."

Following on the theme of interconnectedness and responsibility for all living creatures is the essay "Visiting Norah." Hoagland, who has been sending small sums of money to a grandmother and five orphans in Kampala, Uganda, now decides to meet the family and get to know them. As expected, everyone sees him as a rich American and tries to put the touch on him, but he gets a clearer picture of the struggles they are up against, as well as their resourcefulness. Two other travel essays in the book take him to China and India. Travel encouraged him to find the commonality in people everywhere. Hoagland has felt drawn to visit the Third World not only out of curiosity but to counter the mistakes of the U.S. government, with whose foreign policy he is profoundly at odds. He styles himself a radical dissident, who has widened his "allegiances beyond socialism toward Creation as a whole: salamanders, beech trees, not just auto workers." His travels have an underlying, if bleak, motive: "I want to work out toward the brink of what I think is going to happen—the widespread death of nature, the approaching holocaust of famines, while Westerners retreat in veiled panic into what they prefer to regard as the realer world of cyberspace."

For all his global travel, Hoagland remains a quintessential American, culturally speaking. He did not share the vogue for existential pessimism during the 1950s. "I'd realized World War II had validated Kafka and Camus as my classmates' heartthrobs, but was instead a Whitman fan during the 1950s and ever after, loving every metropolis I encountered as well as the thunderous surf, the rolling landscape." Unlike many nature writers, he continues to be a passionate lover of cities. Hoagland sees himself as following in the footsteps of Emerson and Thoreau. He has been called "our Thoreau," and in an earlier tender essay on that ancestor (and fellow Harvard man), he singled out Thoreau's "playful exactitude" and his "gadfly" dissents. But in this current collection Emerson is cited more often, as inspiration for the conviction that "life is an ecstasy" and perhaps also for the author's packed, peristatic sentences.

The late style of Hoagland essays features long paragraphs that minimize transition; each new paragraph can seem to begin the piece afresh. Time zigzags between past and present in a single sentence. "Giraffes licked salt off my cheeks when I worked in the circus at eighteen and discovered that sweat often coexists with pleasure but that everything should be seen as temporary, with regard to place and glee and colleagues, except I was going to love elephants at a throbbing level as long as I lived." This unitary vision of time posed a problem for his 2001 autobiography *Compass Points*, because we expect more of a narrative arc in memoirs. While it can still be disorienting to attempt to locate the through-line in Hoagland's late pieces, an essay can better accommodate the skipping from one topic to the other. The frank confessional "I" turns on a dime into the generalized "we." The manner is reminiscent of Montaigne's last essays, such as "Of Experience"; like Montaigne, Hoagland now feels he has wisdom to offer, and he is not shy about dispensing it. Whether readers at this moment can sit still and listen to a wisdom dispenser is another matter.

Three kinds of counsel are offered here: the first is drawn from his lifelong experience (the necessity, for instance, "to do no harm and to bear witness")—no less true for being bromidic. The second derives from his deep knowledge of the natural world and informed assessments of the coming ecological threat. The third consists of scattershot jeremiads on the way we live now, such as, "Our secularism powers our recent obsession with longevity, hypochondria and the like. If there is no afterlife, by all means go for the Prozac, Viagra, Botox." Side by side with such tiresome crochets, there are passages in these late essays as good as any Hoagland ever wrote, but the difficulty is sorting the deep from the superficial, in an approach that encourages giving voice to every thought.

Hoagland seems in many ways a writer of the previous, Mailer generation, by virtue of his romanticizing manly types, such as prizefighters, trappers, circus workers and newspapermen, his distrust of the academy, and his tendency to portray women as succoring nurses and ministering sexual angels. In these late essays, he observes himself exchanging the role of randy adventurer for benign protector. "A damsel in distress was a powerful image to my generation. . . . For a long-in-tooth male, the next best thing to sleeping with a much younger woman is to protect her from the machinations of men of her own age." Reflecting on the persistence of mental libido in the waning years, he wonders if he can still exert attraction. "Everybody wants to flee from a dying man, but for the preceding dozen years or more he may exude a certain twilight, or candlelit appeal." Dreaming of one more sexual adventure, he ruefully admits that "my memories are so tangled with the gristle of life that if I try to replay scenes of lovemaking with one of the women I have genuinely loved, it swiftly ramifies into the complexities of the entire relationship— the sadness, the disconnects. The sex in the package cannot be extricated from the stymieing cowardice or passivity, the misperceptions that diluted our passion."

In the essay "Curtain Calls," he phones up his old girlfriends and asks them if they harbor any bad feelings toward him. Was he too stingy when they parted in Istanbul's airport in 1965? he asks an Englishwoman. She laughs and says no, the problem was not money but that he hadn't wished to marry her. In the title essay, we find him asking himself, "Why, I wonder, wasn't sex the best during my marriages, but rather on the sly? Or rotating that around: when and where it was the best, why didn't we simply get married?" This is the kind of thing one might expect someone Hoagland's age to have figured out by now. But there is a sort of naïve bafflement about human relations that he does not want to give up. Short of visiting a psychiatrist (which he refuses to do), he is left to ponder the mystery of his "selfishness, obtuseness, and 'fear and trembling' nevertheless."

Though he insists "I was not really somebody who 'liked animals more than people,'" Hoagland scrutinizes himself and others tentatively, compared to the attention he brings to his animal descriptions. Consider this passage from his famous essay "The Courage of Turtles."

> Turtles cough, burp, whistle, grunt and hiss, and produce social judgments. They put their heads together amicably enough, but then one drives the other back with the suddenness of two dogs who have been conversing in tones too low for an onlooker to hear. They pee in fear when they're first caught, but exercise both pluck and optimism in trying to escape, walking for hundreds of yards within the confines of their pen, carrying the weight of that cumbersome box on legs which are cruelly positioned for walking. They don't feel that the contest is unfair; they keep plugging, like sailorly souls—a bobbing, infirm gait, a brave, sea-legged momentum—stopping occasionally to study the lay of the land.

Here, his boldness, lyricism, and metaphor-making capacities really shine. The persevering turtle can also be seen as a fore-glimpse of the author himself in old age.

In one of those surprising shifts of topic, Hoagland deserts his ruminations on lust, which had threatened to bog down the essay in uncomfortably old-fashioned sexual attitudes, for an utterly charming digression about a visit to his grandchild. He alternates between watching the lordly Hudson River on the train ride down and feeling comically obliged to read every section of the newspaper. He thinks of his newborn grandson, with pleasure, as a "reddish, wiggly, and gloriously amphibious creature," closer to the river creatures than his fellow passengers.

The wounded, lamed soul alluded to earlier has given way to a new benevolence. In his preface to the 1991 story collection, *The Final Fate of the Alligators*, Hoagland wrote that "writers do tend to turn bitter. In fact I can't recall ever meeting a middle-aged writer who wasn't somewhat bitter." Twenty years later, he seems to have surmounted the feeling, writing: "Many people, who seem rather bitter in middle age, by seventy are mainly grateful for having lived, willy-nilly, though quite round-shouldered from having rolled with the punches, and reticently proud of that." It is in his role as grandfather that he seems finally comfortable and at peace with himself: no more running away, ambivalence, "stymieing cowardice." A profession of contentment is a risk for any personal essayist: in a form so dependent on a tense, problematic relation to the self, such benign sentiments can verge on self-satisfaction, and indeed there are some passages here that sound like quiet boasting. But since Hoagland has always excelled at candor, we may give him the benefit of the doubt that he is simply being honest about having achieved fulfillment.

In a summarizing passage that modulates between good and bad news, he tries to balance the debilities of aging with the rewards of understanding: "Loving the earth as it has been, I've believed that heaven is here and the only heaven we have. Perhaps the apprehensiveness old fogies like me feel is not just garden-variety regret at losing former niceties. Yet inconsolable old folks don't last long. A seesaw of fret and opportunity serves them better. Old age is like being posted to a foreign country, where you drop and lose things, misplace names and insights, can't read signage others are guided by. . . . Live with a smile even if you can't spot birds other people are talking about—you've seen them countless times in the past—or are remembering generosities you didn't appreciate sufficiently when your benefactor was alive."

Gratitude has the final word. Edward Hoagland may well live another decade at least, and (we hope) continue to write productively, in which case he may have to develop another subject than the curtain descending. But for now, we are grateful to have this courageous account of a first-rate essayist contemplating the landscape of old age and mortality.

# The Memoir and Its Critics:
## Two Takes

### 1.

The memoir craze in publishing had not gone on long when it began to provoke a backlash and a crisis. The backlash, from various literary critics such as William Gass, James Wolcott, and Susan Sontag, expressed disgust at the narcissism of nobodies, as much as to say, "How dare these neophyte authors think we care about them and their problems?" and a drawing up of skirts from the muck of untransformed experience. That these critics were so distinguished enabled them to get away with such a broad-brush dismissal of dozens of books of variable quality, and their attacks struck a chord because commercial envy had invited a backlash against what seemed merely a fashion. The crisis occurred not from these critics' principled objections but from memoir sales' beginning to decline, indicating that the public itself, having sampled the lives of several dozen representative strangers, was experiencing satiety with the form. Of course, historically speaking, autobiographical writing is too established a literary practice ever to peak or ebb definitively, but the "new memoir" had, for the moment at least, been put on the defensive. It needed some fresh thinking and formal innovation.

Along came David Shields to take up the job with *Remote*.

Refusing to cast his life in the pious scenarios of the recovery movement, with its convenient narrative arc of addiction, denial, revelation, faith, and redemption, he insisted on trying to convey the flotsam and jetsam of daily American experience. Rather than evading the charge of self-absorption with a show of false humility or self-justifying claims of acute suffering leading to triumph, he dove right into the comedy of narcissism, unraveling all its vanities and insecurities. The reader was free to identify (squeamishly, of course) or feel superior. Either way, you could be sure that Shields knew full well what he was doing: a part of him wanted naturally to be loved, another part to provoke and irritate. He courageously played at the borders of acceptance, meanwhile interrogating the autobiographical tradition with references to Rousseau, Nabokov, George Trow, etc. In the end, *Remote* was not so much a memoir in the traditional sense as a meditation on memoirs, and on the pleasures and pitfalls of autobiographical writing in general.

*Remote* was very much a book of its time, but also ahead of its time. It was clearly topical in focusing on America's fascination with celebrity, and the fear that you are not really alive unless the media have fastened their attentions on you. We are shown in these pages the humiliation that people will put themselves through in order to be used by the media. Beyond that, we are brought face-to-face with the deeper, underlying anxiety of self-identity.

What is the nature of the individual self in today's consumer culture? Are our thoughts even our own, or are we merely channeling messages from the mass media, which function as a kind of exoskeleton? Martin Buber wrote, "The perception of one's fellow man as a whole, as a unity, and as unique—even if his wholeness, unity and uniqueness are only partly developed, as is usually the case—is opposed in our time by almost everything that is commonly understood as specifically modern." Shields scrupulously gives appropriate weight to the colonized self, brainwashed by tribal inputs, while at the same time insisting that, yes, we are individuals, in the old humanist sense of the term, if only by virtue of our petty spite, our unresolved desires, and our inexplicable tenderness for the world's detritus.

Shields is a master of the fragment, which allows him to spotlight the isolated geekiness of a particular subject while also weaving thematic links between the pieces. Each fragment may be a mini-essay, a prose poem, a list, a vignette, or some other framing device. The white space between sections permits easy jumps from the personal to the impersonal, the trivial to the lofty. By employing this mosaic technique, Shields operates in an essayistic line that includes Joan Didion and Richard Rodriguez, and that can be traced back to Walter Benjamin's seminal "One-way Street" and "A Berlin Childhood" suites, collaged recollections with speculative analyses about advertising and other modern forms of popular culture. The modernist fragment underscores the lack of coherence and causality in contemporary experience and in the individual self. One might also try to place Shields in his literary generation alongside such madly footnoting, self-reflexive voices as Nicholson Baker, David Foster Wallace, Rick Moody, and Dave Eggers. All these experimental stylists have camped out in the intersection between high and low culture, fiction and nonfiction, reliable witnessing and hypertrophied rationalization. They reflect the postmodern fascination with the uncertainty of any truth.

Shields, too, questions his reliability as a witness by worrying the perspective flaw alluded to in the book's title: emotional remoteness, remote control, and an inability to engage with life. He quotes friends who criticize his character and looks to a series of alter egos whose career trajectories mimic or predict his own. Withal, his persona still comes off as grounded, optimistic, warm, and approachable. In *Remote*, as in Shields's subsequent forays into memoir, such as *Black Planet* (about his identification with African-American professional basketball players), *Enough about You: Adventures in Autobiography,* and *The Thing about Life Is That One Day You'll Be Dead,* we become familiar with certain basic elements of his I-character: his stuttering, Jewishness, obsession with sports and movies, his liberal journalist parents, his awkward adolescence, his graduate school writing apprenticeship, his love affair with Seattle. We also become privy to more minute details, preferences, habits, tics, of such particularity that we almost have to go back to Montaigne to find an equally minuscule self-scrutiny. He confides, for instance, "I prefer previews to the movie, the 'about the author' notes in the back of literary magazines to the contents of the magazine, the pre-game hype to the game. . . . In social situations in which it would be to my disadvantage to appear heterosexual, I attempt to give the impression that it's not beyond my ken to be bisexual. . . . I'm drawn to affectless people whose emptiness is a kind of frozen pond on which I excitedly skate." He shares with Montaigne the conviction that it is precisely these secret little peculiarities, barely acknowledged by oneself, that make a person discretely individual.

By mocking naked self-absorption he almost turns it into its obverse, the dissolution of the ego. That may be why *Remote* seemed ahead of its time when it first appeared in 1996. Since then Shields has become a kind of champion of the memoir and literary nonfiction with his recent manifesto, *Reality Hunger.* I would be less than honest if I did not admit that there is something a little alarming, to me, about the porousness of his identity and the acquisitiveness of his mind, particularly when he appropriates quotes from other writers (including myself). Fragment and collage, at book length, can easily bog down in circularities of repetition. But he seems at least to have found a path out of the redemptive memoir, which is worth celebrating.

2.

What is it about the memoir that, in spite of its many achieve-
ments, it is always forced to stand in the docket? Was it ever
thus, or is it our age that feels especially apologetic and defensive
about this genre? We can only begin reckoning with such questions by first placing the memoir in historical perspective, which
is exactly what Ben Yagoda has done with his timely, useful, and
informative study *Memoir: A History*.

Yagoda, a journalism professor at the University of Delaware,
has written in the past a fine biography, *Will Rogers*, and *About
Town: The New Yorker and the World It Made*, among other books. He
has a lively, resolutely nonacademic, clever style, bordering on
the glib but never less than intelligent. He begins with a few defi-
nitions, sensibly equating the terms "autobiography" and "memoirs" as the attempt "to be a factual account of the author's life,"
adding that "memoir" singular tends to refer to books that cover
only a portion of a life. He then traces the roots of the memoir
from its beginnings in spiritual autobiography and confession
(Saint Augustine, Rousseau), through its many tributaries—the
fictional autobiography (Defoe), the slave narrative, the captivity
narrative, the Victorian memoir of John Stuart Mill and Edmund
Gosse, the criminal/lowlife memoir, the normative memoir (*Life
with Father*), the immigrant memoir, the celebrity memoir, the
addiction/abuse memoir, etc. In an attempt to cover so much territory in three hundred pages, some exemplary works are bound
to be overlooked (I particularly missed Casanova, the duc de
Saint-Simon, Alexander Herzen, V. S. Naipaul, and all of Japanese I-literature). But for all that, his book is well researched and
clearly organized.

In assessing the problematic aspects of memoir, Yagoda
focuses on lies, intentional and not. As he shows, rather than

a recent fad, autobiographies have been popular for centuries, and there have been autobiographical hoaxes for just as long. "In any society where a particular currency has high value and is fairly easily fashioned, counterfeiters will quickly and inevitably emerge," he writes. This is so unassailably true that it makes you wonder why the educated public can still be so shocked each time a sham memoir surfaces. There are liars and rogues in every profession; why not literature? To prove his point Yagoda enumerates the many charlatans who faked their memoirs; while this is good fun up to a point, it does get repetitious. Much fresher, to my mind, is his synthesis of the psychological research about memory's distortions. It appears that even when we want to tell the truth, we get the facts wrong. Modern thinkers such as Freud, Wittgenstein, and William James have added their skepticism about our ability to rise above subjective rationalization and give a reliable account of our own experience.

Perhaps a more snobbish objection to the memoir is that it is too inclusive, disregarding class distinctions and other claims to authority. The ever-receptive William Dean Howells, Yagoda writes, said that autobiographical books were " 'the most delightful of all reading,' in large part because they constituted the most democratic province of the republic of letters." On the other hand, William Gass's antimemoir screed takes the more exclusionary road in demanding, "Why is it so exciting to say, now that everyone knows it anyway, 'I was born . . . I was born . . . I was born?' I pooped in my pants, I was betrayed, I made straight A's." If that were all the best memoirs said, of course, Gass would be right, but it is noteworthy how many educated people nodded in agreement at his broad-brush attack.

Yagoda himself is not exactly a champion of the memoir. He cracks up at bogus contemporary examples, such as ones about alien abductions or "a preacher who says he was hit by a truck, saw heaven, and came back to life." He cannot get enough of quoting with a superior chuckle the plot summaries from *Through a Woman's I: An Annotated Biography of American Women's Autobiographical Writings, 1946–1976*. Though he tries to be evenhanded in citing both defenders and detractors of the memoir, his own condescending prejudice comes disturbingly through. He seems convinced it is intrinsically inferior to fiction, as when he aphorizes, "Memoir is to fiction as photography is to painting, also in being easier to do well." A highly debatable point: if it were so easy to do well, the form would have fewer detractors. His highest compliment, paid to Primo Levi, is that *The Periodic Table* displays "a sense of language and form equal to the finest fiction." Why not say about a good novel that it is written as well as the finest memoirs? If he comes down finally on the side of the memoir, it is just barely: "The memoir boom, for all its sins, has been a net plus for the cause of writing. Under its auspices, voices and stories have emerged that, otherwise, would have been dull impersonal nonfiction tomes or forgettable autobiographical novels, or wouldn't have been expressed at all." Faint praise indeed, especially alongside the patronizing notion that the genre has mostly performed the service of documenting the lives of otherwise mediocre writers.

Missing from such assessments is an appreciation for just how difficult it is to make genuine literary art out of autobiographical materials, precisely because the would-be memoirist is swamped with too much data at the outset. The successful memoirist requires powers of imagination and form of a different but not weaker order than those who fashion made-up stories.

Maybe because Yagoda is a literary journalist, he seems always on the track of the juicy scandal, the huge best seller or colossal flop, and less attuned to the lonely miracle of exquisite prose. For instance, here is how he dispenses with two of the greatest English autobiographical works of the nineteenth century: "In 1821, Wordsworth's onetime protégé Thomas De Quincey created a scandal with his anonymous *Confessions of an English Opium Eater,* which is exactly what it says it is. Two years later, the prominent man of letters William Hazlitt wrote an embarrassing narrative of his disastrous infatuation with a nineteen-year-old waitress; he published it anonymously, under the title *Liber Amoris,* but didn't fool anybody. (Nor was it greeted with enthusiasm: one review called it a 'wretched compound of folly and nauseous sensibility'; another stated that it 'mixed filth and utter despicableness.')" Never mind that De Quincey's labyrinthine prose remains a monumental stylistic achievement or that Hazlitt generously raised the stakes for candid, warts-and-all self-portraiture. Similarly, Richard Wright's *Black Boy,* one of the most powerful American autobiographies ever written, is discussed only in terms of the cowardly publisher's decision to sever the final sections about the Communist Party from the main body of the work.

In explaining that space limits made it impossible to discuss certain works he himself considers great memoirs, such as Vladimir Nabokov's *Speak, Memory* or Mary McCarthy's *Memories of a Catholic Girlhood,* he writes, "Pride of place goes to books that memorably or notably did a significant thing first, and that changed the way the genre was conceived." I would argue that Nabokov and McCarthy did break new ground, the former by his distinguished lyrical prose, and the latter by the risks she took in making her I-character obnoxious. Also, both books consist of strings of discrete personal essays that add up to a memoir, a formal innovation in itself. Yagoda says nothing about the fertile relationship of the memoir to the personal essay, which is a pity, considering that some of the greatest works of autobiographical prose are personal essays. Of course, Yagoda has every right to compose a brisk historical survey of the genre, rather than getting bogged down in literary criticism. The catch is that significant "firsts" and literary greatness are not so easily disentangled.

Yagoda is strongest on taxonomies, such as his definition of what he calls "shtick" lit: "that is to say, books perpetrated by people who undertook an unusual project with the express purpose of writing about it." He can be cavalier when it comes to individual cases, as when he mistakenly lumps Lorna Sage's wryly amusing, elegantly wrought *Bad Blood* in the category of the English "misery memoir" that tells "tales of extreme woe" about childhood. Perhaps, too, if he had been more attentive to some other recent memoirs that go unmentioned, such as Vivian Gornick's *Fierce Attachments*, Emily Fox Gordon's *Mockingbird Years*, Jill Ciment's *Half a Life*, or Saïd Sayrafiezadeh's *When Skateboards Will Be Free*, he might have seen that much more balance and self-mocking perspective is available to the coming-of-age memoir than simply slotting it into the category of trauma and misery would suggest. Broadly speaking, given all the risks of distortion and self-serving, many memoirists still manage to get it right: to reach a deeper level of self-insight and detachment that enables them to turn their "I" into a believable, flawed character, and to situate that "I" within the proper proportions of self and world. About that standard, Yagoda says far too little. He is less interested in dispelling misgivings about the memoir than in compiling them for a breezy read. In doing so, he reflects the attitudes of the literary establishment, which still turns up its nose at this honorable genre while refusing to acknowledge the degree to which egotism, stylistic mediocrity, and self-serving opportunism are just as prevalent in fiction, poetry, and all the other genres of written expression.

# Acknowledgments

Some of these essays originally appeared, in similar or altered form, in *The Ohio Review, Writing Creative Non-Fiction* (edited by Carolyn Forche and Philip Gerard), *The Fourth Genre, Salmagundi, Creative Nonfiction, The Harvard Educational Review, Seneca Review, Writers and Their Notebooks* (edited by Diana M. Raab), *The Writers' Chronicle, Gulf Coast, Harper's, The Teachers and Writers Guide to Classic American Literature, The New York Review of Books,* and *Bookforum.* I'm grateful to all these publications; a special thanks for their meticulous editing to Hattie Fletcher at *Creative Nonfiction,* Donovan Hoen at *Harper's,* and Robert Silvers at *The New York Review of Books.*

My deepest gratitude goes to my students, for their keen insight, talent, enthusiasm and challenging questions. Without them this book would never have come about. I'm indebted to the Civitella Ranieri Foundation, its gracious director, Dana Prescott and hospitable staff, for providing me with a month's retreat in beautiful Umbria that allowed me the tranquility to finish this collection.

I can't thank enough my literary agent, Wendy Weil, for her lifelong (forty years') support. She passed away, tragically, in September, but not before she found me the perfect home for my book at Free Press, reuniting me with estimable publisher Martha Levin. I've been blessed with a very skillful, shrewd, sympathetic editor, Millicent Bennett, and her able assistant, Chloe Perkins.

As always, I tested early versions of these pieces on friends and colleagues—Robert and Peg Boyers, Vivian Gornick, Patricia Hampl, Lis Harris, Margo Jefferson, Allison Jones, David Lazar, Richard Locke, Honor Moore, Patricia O'Toole, Scott Russell Sanders, Vijay Seshadri, Michael Steinberg, and Mark Street—who were kind enough to respond with a blend of diplomacy and honesty.

Finally, a big thank-you to my wife, Cheryl, and daughter, Lily, for their love, good humor, and forbearance.

# Reading List

What follows is a list of suggested readings: very roughly speaking, a canon. Though it may appear dauntingly long at first, it is by no means all-inclusive, nor is it meant to be. What it does reflect, perhaps to a fault, is my own reading in and intuitions about the field of nonfiction. I am well aware that there are many gaps as well as debatable inclusions below. But I offer the list as a starting point; others can fine-tune it to their taste. Its main purpose is to convey the richness, variety, and depth of literary nonfiction. For those who are confused about what can or cannot be done in this genre, and how to do it (which means practically everyone), I would submit that the answers reside less in prescriptive tips and how-to manuals than in immersive reading. If you are writing a memoir, for instance, you do not have to reinvent the wheel. There are precedents galore that can both instruct and empower. Nor is it necessary or advisable to restrict your reading to autobiographies, personal essays, and whatever passes for creative nonfiction: once you have grasped that there are wonderful prose writers in every field under the sun—articulate, expressive, cultivated practitioners—you can better figure out how to expand your focus from the personal to the world-embracing.

## Some Classic Autobiographies and Memoirs (Pre–Twentieth Century)

Saint Augustine: *Confessions*

Benvenuto Cellini: *Autobiography*

Jacques Casanova: *Memoirs*

Duc de Saint-Simon: *Memoirs*

Margaret Cavendish, Duchess of Newcastle: *Memoirs, Life of the Duke*

Jean-Jacques Rousseau: *Confessions*

Benjamin Franklin: *Autobiography*

Johann Wolfgang von Goethe: *Autobiography* ("Poetry and Truth")

François-René Chateaubriand: *Mémoires d'outre tombe*

Stendhal: *Memoirs of an Egotist* and *The Life of Henri Brulard*

John Stuart Mill: *Autobiography*

Frederick Douglass: *Autobiography*

Henry David Thoreau: *Walden*

Harriet Jacobs: *Incidents in the Life of a Slave-Girl*

Thomas De Quincey: *Confessions of an English Opium-Eater*

John Ruskin: *Praeterita*

Alexander Herzen: *My Past and Thoughts*

Edmund Gosse: *Father and Son*

Daniel Paul Schreber: *Memoirs of My Nervous Illness*

Ulysses S. Grant: *Memoirs*

## Some Early Twentieth-century Memoirs

Henry Adams: *The Education of Henry Adams*

Virginia Woolf: "A Sketch of the Past" (in *Moments of Being*)

Richard Wright: *Black Boy* and *American Hunger*

André Gide: *If It Die* and *Madeleine*

W. E. B. Du Bois: *The Autobiography*

Frank Harris: *My Life and Loves*

H. G. Wells: *Experiment in Autobiography*
T. E. Lawrence: *The Seven Pillars of Wisdom*
Agnes Smedley: *Daughter of Earth*
Henri Michaux: *Miserable Miracle*
H. L. Mencken: *Happy Days, Newspaper Days, Heathen Days*
Leon Trotsky: *Autobiography*
Mohandas K. Gandhi: *Autobiography*
Mikhail Zoshchenko: *Before Sunrise*
Robert Graves: *Goodbye to All That*
Victor Serge: *Memoirs of a Revolutionary*

## Some Postwar Twentieth-century Memoirs

Nirad Chaudhuri: *The Autobiography of an Unknown Indian*
Mary McCarthy: *Memoirs of a Catholic Girlhood*
Vladimir Nabokov: *Speak, Memory*
Edward Dahlberg: *Because I Was Flesh*
J. R. Ackerley: *My Father and Myself* and *My Dog Tulip*
Jean-Paul Sartre: *The Words*
Nadezhda Mandelstam: *Hope against Hope*
Primo Levi: *Survival in Auschwitz, The Reawakening*
Carlos Levi: *Christ Stopped at Eboli*
Ernst Junger: *The Storm of Steel*
Natalia Ginzburg: *Family Sayings*
Storm Jameson: *Journey from the North*
Malcolm X: *The Autobiography*
Frederick Exley: *A Fan's Notes*
Christopher Isherwood: *Christopher and His Kind, My Guru and His Disciple*
Czeslaw Milosz: *Native Realm*
Victor Shklovsky: *A Sentimental Journey, Third Factory*
Thomas Bernhard: *The Cause, The Cellar, The Breath* (3 vol. autobiography)

V. S. Pritchett: *A Cab at the Door*

Elias Canetti: *The Tongue Set Free, The Torch in My Ear, The Play of the Eyes*

Konstantin Paustovsky: *The Story of a Life*

Boris Pasternak: *Safe Conduct, I Remember*

C. G. Jung: *Memories, Dreams and Reflections*

Kate Simon: *Bronx Primitive*

Lewis Mumford: *Sketches from Life*

Loren Eiseley: *All the Strange Hours*

Thomas Merton: *The Seven-Storey Mountain*

Colette: *My Mother's House*

Michel Leiris: *Manhood, Rules of the Game*

Geoffrey Wolff: *The Duke of Deception*

Hilary Masters: *Last Stands*

Frank Conroy: *Stop-Time*

Peter Handke: *A Sorrow beyond Dreams*

John Updike: *Self-Consciousness*

Anatole Broyard: *Kafka Was the Rage, Intoxicated by My Illness*

V. S. Naipaul: "Prologue to an Autobiography," *The Enigma of Arrival*

Chester Himes: *The Quality of Hurt*

Luis Buñuel: *My Last Sigh*

Elia Kazan: *A Life*

Sylvia Ashton-Warner: *Teacher*

Nelson Mandela: *Long Walk to Freedom*

Gregor von Rezzori: *The Snows of Yesteryear*

## Recent Memoirs

Philip Roth: *Patrimony*

Vivian Gornick: *Fierce Attachments*

Richard Rodriguez: *Hunger of Memory*

Lucy Grealy: *Autobiography of a Face*

Joanne Beard: *The Boys of My Youth*

Mary Karr: *The Liar's Club*
Frank McCourt: *Angela's Ashes, Teacher Man*
Dave Eggers: *A Heartbreaking Work of Staggering Genius*
Doris Lessing: *Under My Skin, Walking in the Shade*
Amos Oz: *A Tale of Love and Darkness*
Art Spiegelman: *Maus*
Marjane Satrapi: *Persepolis* 1 and 2
David Shields: *Remote*
Emily Fox Gordon: *Mockingbird Years*
Lorna Sage: *Bad Blood*
Spalding Gray: *Swimming to Cambodia*
Jill ker-Conway: *The Road from Corain*
Elizabeth Kendall: *American Daughter*
J. M. Coetzee: *Boyhood, Youth*
Geoff Dyer: *Out of Sheer Rage*
Paula Fox: *Borrowed Finery*
James Salter: *Burning the Days*
Edmund de Waal: *The Hare with Amber Eyes*
Paul Auster: *The Invention of Solitude, Winter Journal*
Alison Bechdel: *Fun Home*

## Some Classic Essayists

Seneca: *Letters from a Stoic*
Plutarch: *Selected Essays on Love, the Family and the Good Life*
Cicero: *Selected Works, On the Good Life*
Michel de Montaigne: *Complete Essays*
Francis Bacon: *Essays*
Abraham Cowley: *Essays, Plays and Sundry Verses*
Samuel Johnson: Essays from *The Rambler, The Idler, The Adventurer*
Joseph Addison and Richard Steele: *The Tatler and the Spectator*
Charles Lamb: *Essays of Elia* and *The Last Essays of Elia*

William Hazlitt: *Selected Essays*
Leigh Hunt: *Essays, Autobiography*
Thomas De Quincey: *Selected Essays*
Charles Dickens: *Sketches from Boz*
Ralph Waldo Emerson: *Essays*
Robert Louis Stevenson: *The Lantern Bearers and Other Essays*
Oscar Wilde: *De Profundis, Selected Essays*
Matthew Arnold: *Culture and Anarchy*
Walter Pater: *The Renaissance, Appreciations*
Thomas Carlyle: *Sartor Resartus*, "On Heroes and Hero-Worship"
Oliver Wendell Holmes: *The Autocrat of the Breakfast Table*

## Some Twentieth-century Essayists

Max Beerbohm: *Selected Prose*
G. K. Chesterton: *Tremendous Trifles*
Hilaire Belloc: *On Nothing, On Everything, On Anything, On
    Something*
Virginia Woolf: *Collected Essays, The Death of the Moth*
George Orwell: *Collected Essays*
James Baldwin: *Collected Essays, Notes of a Native Son, The Fire
    Next Time*
Robert Benchley: *The Benchley Roundup*
James Thurber: *Writings and Drawings*
H. L. Mencken: *A Mencken Chrestomathy, Prejudices* (vols. 1–6)
S. J. Perelman: *The Best of S. J. Perelman*
F. Scott Fitzgerald: *The Crack-Up*
A. J. Liebling: *Just Enough Liebling*
Walter Benjamin: *Illuminations, Reflections*
Susan Sontag: *Against Interpretation, Under the Sign of Saturn*
E. B. White: *Selected Essays*
C. L. R. James: *The C. L. R. James Reader*
Seymour Krim: *What Is This Cat's Story?*

Jorge Luis Borges: *Collected Non-Fictions*
Czeslaw Milosz: *To Begin Again*
M. F. K. Fisher: *The Gastronomical Me, The Art of Eating*
Osamu Dazai: *Self Portraits*
Natalia Ginzburg: *The Little Virtues, A Place to Live*
Roland Barthes: *Mythologies, Barthes on Barthes*
Hubert Butler: *Independent Spirit*
Joseph Brodsky: *Less Than One*
Guy Davenport: *The Geography of the Imagination, The Hunter
    Gracchus*
Gore Vidal: *United States: Essays 1952–1992*

## Some Contemporary Essayists (Personal, Familiar, and Humorist)

Joan Didion: *Slouching toward Bethlehem, The White Album*
Edward Hoagland: *Heart's Desire, Sex and the River Styx*
Annie Dillard: *Pilgrim at Tinker's Creek, Teaching a Stone to Talk*
Joseph Epstein: *The Middle of My Tether*
Adrienne Rich: *On Lies, Secrets, and Silence*
Vivian Gornick: *Approaching Eye Level, The Situation and the Story*
William Gass: *On Being Blue*
Phillip Lopate: *Getting Personal, Notes on Sontag*
Nancy Mairs: *Plaintext, Waist-High in the World*
Scott Russell Sanders: *The Paradise of Bombs*
Gerald Early: *Tuxedo Junction*
Daniel Harris: *The Rise and Fall of Gay Culture*
Anne Fadiman: *Ex Libris*
David Sedaris: *Naked*
Sara Suleri: *Meatless Days*
Lynn Freed: *Reading, Writing, and Leaving Home*
Jonathan Lethem: *The Disappointment Artist*
John D'Agata: *Halls of Fame, The Lost Origins of the Essay*

Emily Fox Gordon: *Book of Days*
Lia Purpura: *Rough Likeness*
Eula Biss: *Notes from No Man's Land*
Siri Hustvedt: *Living, Thinking, Looking*

## Nature, Science, Medicine, and the Environment

Richard Jeffries: *The Life of the Fields*
J. Henri Fabre: *Fabre's Book of Insects*
John Muir: *The Mountains of California*
Charles Darwin: *The Voyage of the Beagle, On the Origin of Species*
William Bartram: *Travels and Other Writings*
John James Audubon: *Writings and Drawings*
John Burroughs: *Birch Browsings*
Aldo Leopold: *Sand County Almanac*
Henry Beston: *The Outermost House*
Edward Abbey: *Desert Solitaire*
Loren Eiseley: *The Immense Journey, The Night Country*
Stephen Jay Gould: *The Panda's Thumb*
Lewis Thomas: *The Lives of a Cell: Notes of a Biology Watcher*
F. González-Crussi: *Notes of an Anatomist*
Oliver Sacks: *The Man Who Mistook His Wife for a Hat, An Anthropologist on Mars*
A. R. Luria: *The Mind of a Mnemonist, The Man with a Shattered World*
Richard Selzer: *Mortal Lessons: Notes on the Art of Surgery*
Gretel Ehrlich: *The Solace of Open Spaces*
John McPhee: *Coming into the Country*
Peter Matthiessen: *The Snow Leopard*
Wendell Berry: *The Unsettling of America: Culture and Agriculture*
Edward Hoagland: *Hoagland on Nature*
Barry Lopez: *Arctic Dreams*
Michael Pollan: *Second Nature, The Botany of Desire*

## Psychology

Sigmund Freud: *The Wolf Man, Dora, Civilization and Its Discontents*
D. W. Winnicott: *Winnicott on the Child, Playing and Reality*
Karen Horney: *Feminine Psychology*
Leslie H. Farber: *The Ways of the Will*
Adam Phillips: *On Kissing, Tickling, and Being Bored*
Jules Henry: *Pathways to Madness*

## Architecture and Landscape

Lewis Mumford: *Sidewalk Critic, The Lewis Mumford Reader*
Ada Louise Huxtable: *On Architecture*
Jane Jacobs: *The Death and Life of Great American Cities*
J. B. Jackson: *Landscape in Sight*
William H. Whyte: *The Essential William H. Whyte*
Robert Venturi, Denise Scott Brown, and Steven Izenour: *Learning from Las Vegas*

## Dance

Edwin Denby: *Dancers, Buildings and People in the Streets*
Arlene Croce: *Croce on Dance, The Fred and Ginger Book*
Elizabeth Kendall: *Where She Danced*

## Art

Denis Diderot: *Diderot on Art*
John Ruskin: *The Stones of Venice*
Harold Rosenberg: *Discovering the Present*
Clement Greenberg: *Collected Essays and Criticism*
Meyer Schapiro: *Impressionism, Modern Art*
Robert Smithson: *The Collected Writings*

John Berger: *Ways of Seeing, Selected Essays*
Robert Hughes: *Nothing If Not Critical*

## Sports

Red Smith: *The Red Smith Reader, To Absent Friends*
A. J. Liebling: *The Sweet Science*
Roger Angell: *The Summer Game, Five Seasons*
Gay Talese: *The Silent Season of a Hero*

## Literary Criticism and Appreciation

Samuel Taylor Coleridge: *Biographia Literaria*
Virginia Woolf: *The Common Reader*
D. H. Lawrence: *Studies in American Literature*
W. H. Auden: *The Dyer's Hand, Forewords and Afterwords*
John Berryman: *The Freedom of the Poet*
Randall Jarrell: *The First [Second, Third] Book of Criticism*
Alfred Kazin: *On Native Grounds*
Cynthia Ozick: *Art and Ardor, Quarrel & Quandary*
Edmund Wilson: *Axel's Castle, The Shores of Light, Patriotic Gore*
Lionel Trilling: *The Liberal Imagination, The Opposing Self*
Elizabeth Hardwick: *Bartleby in Manhattan and Other Essays*
David Shields: *Reality Hunger*
Geoff Dyer: *Out of Sheer Rage*
Lynne Sharon Schwartz: *Ruined by Reading*
Patricia Hampl: *I Could Tell You Stories*

## Film

Otis Ferguson: *The Film Criticism of Otis Ferguson*
James Agee: *Agee on Film*
Manny Farber: *Negative Space*
Robert Warshow: *The Immediate Experience*

André Bazin: *What Is Cinema?* vols. 1–2
Parker Tyler: *Screening the Sexes, Magic and Myth in the Movies*
Pauline Kael: *For Keeps*
Andrew Sarris: *Confessions of a Cultist, Politics and Cinema*
Stanley Cavell: *Pursuits of Happiness*

## Music and Drama

William Hazlitt: *Hazlitt on Theatre*
George Bernard Shaw: *Music in London, Our Theatres in the Nineties*
Hector Berlioz: *Evenings with the Orchestra*
Max Beerbohm: *Around Theatres*
Wayne Koestenbaum: *The Queen's Throat*
Margo Jefferson: *On Michael Jackson*
John Jeremiah Johnson: *Pulphead*
Charles Rosen: *The Classical Style, The Romantic Generation*

## Political and Social Writing

Niccolò Macchiavelli: *The Prince*
Mary Wollstonecraft: *A Vindication of the Rights of Woman*
Edmund Burke: *On Empire, Liberty, and Reform*
Alexis de Tocqueville: *Democracy in America*
William Cobbett: *Rural Rides*
Karl Marx: *The Eighteenth Brumaire of Louis Bonaparte*
Rebecca West: *Black Lamb and Grey Falcon*
Antonio Gramsci: *Letters from Prison*
George Orwell: *The Road to Wigan Pier, Homage to Catalonia*
James Agee: *Let Us Now Praise Famous Men*
Edmund Wilson: *To the Finland Station*
Hannah Arendt: *The Origins of Totalitarianism, The Human
    Condition*
Simone de Beauvoir: *The Second Sex*

Eldridge Cleaver: *Soul on Ice*
Michael Herr: *Dispatches*
Norman Mailer: *Armies of the Night*

## Philosophical, Moral, Religious, and Other Treatises

Marcus Aurelius: *The Meditations*
Erasmus: *In Praise of Folly, The Adages*
Pascal: *Pensées*
Stendhal: *On Love*
Friedrich Nietzsche: *The Genealogy of Morals, Beyond Good
    and Evil*
Simone Weil: *The Need for Roots, Waiting for God*
E. M. Cioran: *The Temptation to Exist*
Gaston Bachelard: *The Poetics of Space, The Poetics of Reverie*
Theodor Adorno: *Minima Moralia*

## Diaries and Notebooks

Sei Shonagon: *The Pillow Book*
Kenko: *Essays in Idleness*
Samuel Pepys: *The Diary of Samuel Pepys*
James Boswell: *Journals*
Ralph Waldo Emerson: *The Notebooks*
Edmond and Jules de Goncourt: *Journals*
George Templeton Strong: *The Diaries*
Franz Kafka: *Diaries*
Anne Frank: *The Diary of Anne Frank*
Victor Klemperer: *I Shall Bear Witness*
Cesare Pavese: *The Burning Brand*
Witold Gombrowicz: *Diary*, vols. 1–3
André Gide: *Journals*

## Letters

Mme. de Sévigné: *Letters to Her Daughter*
Alexander Pushkin: *Collected Letters*
Lord Byron: *Byron's Letters and Journals*
John Keats: *Selected Letters*
Gustave Flaubert: *Selected Letters*
Vincent van Gogh: *Dear Theo*
Franz Kafka: *Letters to Milena*

## Aphorisms, Thought Catch-Alls, and Similar Curiosities

La Rochefoucauld: *Maxims*
La Bruyère: *Characters*
Robert Burton: *The Anatomy of Melancholy*
Thomas Browne: *The Urn Burial, Religio Medici*
Giacomo Leopardi: *Pensieri*
Cyril Connolly (Palinaurus): *The Unquiet Grave*
Yang Ye (editor): *Vignettes from the Late Ming*

## History

Thucydides: *The Peloponnesian War*
Herodotus: *The Histories*
Edward Gibbon: *The Decline and Fall of the Roman Empire*
Thomas Carlyle: *The French Revolution*
Jules Michelet: *Histories of France*
Washington Irving: *A History of New York*
Jacob Burckhardt: *The Civilization of the Renaissance in Italy*
Henry Adams: *History of the United States under Jefferson and Madison*
Francis Parkman: *France and England in North America, The Oregon Trail*

Richard Hofstadter: *The Age of Reform, Anti-Intellectualism in American Life*

Ferdinand Braudel: *The Mediterranean*

## Biographies

Plutarch: *Lives of the Greeks and Romans*
Giorgio Vasari: *Lives of the Artists*
John Aubrey: *Brief Lives*
Samuel Johnson: *Lives of the English Poets*
James Boswell: *Life of Samuel Johnson*
Elizabeth Gaskell: *The Life of Charlotte Brontë*
Charles Sainte-Beuve: *Portraits*
J. Anthony Froude: *Thomas Carlyle*
Lytton Strachey: *Eminent Victorians*
Gertrude Stein: *The Autobiography of Alice B. Toklas*
Geoffrey Scott: *Portrait of Zélide*

## Travel and Place

Basho: *Back Roads to Far Towns*
Johann Wolfgang von Goethe: *Italian Journey*
Frances Trollope: *Domestic Manners of the Americans*
Astolfe de Custine: *Letters from Russia*
Charles M. Doughty: *Travels in Arabia Deserta*
Robert Louis Stevenson: *Travels with a Donkey*
Mark Twain: *Life on the Mississippi*
Richard F. Burton: *First Footsteps in East Africa, Wanderings in West Africa*
Henry James: *Collected Travel Writings*
Robert Byron: *The Road to Oxiana*
Djuna Barnes: *New York*
Osip Mandelstam: *Journey to Armenia*

Theodore Dreiser: *The Color of a Great City*

Paul Morand: *New York*

Joseph Roth: *What I Saw, Report from a Parisian Paradise*

Louis Aragon: *Paris Peasant*

D. H. Lawrence: *Twilight in Sicily, Sea and Sardinia, Mornings in Mexico*

Eleanor Clark: *Rome and a Villa*

Mary McCarthy: *The Stones of Florence, Venice Observed*

Claude Lévi-Strauss: *Tristes Tropiques*

Joseph Mitchell: *Up in the Old Hotel*

John McNulty: *This Place on Third Avenue*

John Graves: *Goodbye to a River*

Bruce Chatwin: *In Patagonia*

Ryszard Kapuściński: *The Emperor, Another Day of Life, The Shadow of the Sun*

Patrick Leigh Fermor: *A Time of Gifts, Between the Woods and the Water*

Benjamin Taylor: *Naples Declared*

# About the Author

**Phillip Lopate** is the author of *Against Joie de Vivre, Portrait of My Body*, and *Being with Children*, among other books. A recipient of the Guggenheim and National Endowment for the Arts fellowships, his works have appeared in *Best American Essays, The Paris Review, The New York Times*, and many other publications. He lives in Brooklyn, New York, with his wife and daughter, and directs the graduate nonfiction program at Columbia University.